DAILY DEVOTIONAL series

WISDOM
HUNTERS

SEEKING
GOD
IN THE
PROVERBS

90 READINGS FOR
INSPIRATION, INTIMACY & INSTRUCTION

BOYD BAILEY

DEDICATION

ANDY STANLEY

MY FRIEND, MY PASTOR,
AND THE WISEST PERSON I KNOW.

WALK WITH THE WISE AND BECOME WISE.

PROVERBS 13:20

ACKNOWLEDGEMENTS

Thank you, **Rita,**
for asking me, "Is this the wise thing to do?"

Thank you, **JT, Tripp,** and **Todd,**
for being sons-in-law who walk with the wise!

Thank you, **George Morgan,**
for a life that modeled daily meditation on the Proverbs.

Thank you, **Donna Reed, Susan White,** and **Lee McCutchan,**
for your expert editing.

Thank you, **Charlie** and **Patty Renfroe,**
for being mentors who exemplify wise decision making.

Thank you, **Steve Reed,**
for instructing me in wisdom,
especially the seven years we traveled together.

Thank you,
Lanny Donoho, Mike Kendrick, Woody Faulk, and **Joel Manby,**
for ten years of accountability in wise decision making.

TESTIMONIES

Experiencing God stories from the Wisdom Hunters devotional writings:

Come to Me
Thank you so much for this word, which I believe was right on time. Many things are going on with my life right now; so many things are troubling me. It is like Jesus is talking through the pages of this message. Thank you again.
Debbie

Be Yourself
Dear Wisdom Hunters,
I have been receiving your devotionals for over a year now, and they have truly been a blessing to me and my family and friends as well. It seems like the writer knows exactly what is going on in my life. I know God is speaking to me through these devotionals. My husband and I are going through some very difficult times right now, and the only thing that has kept me going is the inspirational encouragement that I receive through Wisdom Hunters. I just want to thank you. God is moving through your words, which are being sent all over the United States. God bless you!
Sonja

Perseverance Pattern
I just discovered your link to easily accessing previous devotionals, which is an awesome feature, and decided to reread this one. It was exactly what I needed, and I feel very strengthened by it! I praise God for directing me to your ministry and start each day by reading your devotionals. Thank you so much for your faithful work and rich blessing toward my spiritual growth!
Wendy

TESTIMONIES

Wise Living

*Wow! Thank you. This is just what I needed to hear right at this moment.
This is truly God talking directly to me as if this were an appointment with Him.
My husband goes to church with me every Sunday and even serves, but he does
not like to talk with me about God. I guess maybe I get too excited and pushy
or preachy. I so wish someday we can read the Bible or pray together.
Thank you so much for the article. I will print and study it.*

Lucy

Purpose Fulfillment

*I read this with tears and at the same time joy for the encouragement that,
in spite of my sin, our Lord would still see me worthy of fulfilling His purpose for
my life. I want nothing more and nothing less than this. I am sincerely thankful.*

Ann

Promise Land Spirit

*I love this devotional! The Lord gave me the word go for my one-word focus for
this year, and this says everything He keeps telling me. Thanks for writing this!
I am going to link to this post on my blog Saturday. Continued blessings to you
for following where God has led you.*

Debbie

Hot for God

*This is so beautiful to me. Thank you so much for your words of wisdom.
You inspire me every day to stay strong in my love of Jesus! I am hot for God.
Blessings to you and your family. Happy New Year!*

Grace

TESTIMONIES

Night before Christmas

I want to thank you for this ministry of great encouragement and truth that God has given you. I found Wisdom Hunters as a link on Family Christian web site. Now, however, I have bookmarked it by itself and go directly to you each morning as part of my morning devotional. The encouragement and truth a believer receives here are not to be underestimated. Peace and grace.

Carl

Delayed Joy

Thank you for your wise words in helping me to see God-breathed Scripture in a new light! Many thanks for helping me through the most difficult journey in my life (so far) as a single woman with Lyme disease and home confined for the last ten years. I will no longer hang on to being "realistic" as my doctors put it. I will try not to put limits on what God can still do in my life. I will pray and ask for the faith to believe that God can restore my health and that He can provide me with the love of a God-fearing husband and maybe even a child someday! His power and love have no boundaries! Praise be to God for His love and desire to commune with our souls! Boyd, your words have renewed my hope! I have read these Scriptures dozens of times over the years. We all need our faith renewed from time to time. So thank you for being the Lord's messenger today and every day!

Michelle

PREFACE

Seeking God in the Proverbs is a collection
of the reader's favorites from the daily Wisdom Hunters
e-mail devotionals written between 2008 and 2009.

These flow from my heart as I have wept and rejoiced with the Lord
in my daily quiet times. I pray the Lord will use these writings to bring
inspiration, intimacy, and instruction to your relationship with Him.

A Servant in Christ,
Boyd Bailey

boyd@wisdomhunters.com

BOOKS BY BOYD BAILEY

E-BOOK DEVOTIONALS AND PRINT BOOKS
Infusion: A 90-day Devotional
Seeking Daily the Heart of God: A 365-day Devotional
Seeking Daily the Heart of God, Volume II: A 365-day Devotional
Seeking God in Psalms: A 90-day Devotional
Wisdom for Marriage: A 30-day Devotional
Wisdom for Grads: A 30-day Devotional
Wisdom for Mothers: A 30-day Devotional
Wisdom for Fathers: A 30-day Devotional

All books and devotionals available at wisdomhunters.com

INTRODUCTION

Wisdom is what every God-fearing person wants. The Lord has put in the heart of His disciples a desire to live life from His perspective. Indeed, a heart of wisdom is ever growing, as a follower of Jesus seeks to know Him and understand His Word. Wisdom hunting is a process of humble learning that lasts a lifetime. The wise never arrive in their acquisition of God's knowledge, wisdom, and principles for living. Students seek wisdom.

When I was thirty-one years old, a friend described to me his wisdom journey. I listened intently because his life was worth emulating. He was the spiritual leader of his family, a respected businessman, and a student of the Scriptures. Astonishingly, for ten years he daily read a chapter in Proverbs based on the day of the month. For example, on May 3 he read the third chapter of Proverbs and mediated on its meaning for his life.

I felt the Holy Spirit prompting me to accept that same challenge; so from age thirty-one to age forty-one, I read a chapter in Proverbs based on the day of the month. It was uncanny how what I was learning mirrored my life experiences. Everything from the wise management of money to avoiding sexual temptation transformed my behavior. Ideas about parenting, marriage, and relationships began to strongly motivate my selfless service to others.

The other very real reality about practicing the principles of Proverbs is it works. If we humbly and consistently follow these extremely practical teachings, we grow in Christ's character. Once the Holy Spirit illumines our mind to understand the enormous benefit in behaving out the Lord's principles, we are then responsible to embed them into our behavior. Knowledge without application only contributes to pseudo spirituality that lacks life.

So we struggle together to be consistent with honest speech, kind attitudes, humble service, and sharing the truth in love. Like an athlete in training, we work hard at developing godly habits—indeed, it is painful and frustrating at times—but we stay the course of character development for Christ's sake. Proverbs applied produces faith fruit.

INTRODUCTION

I am grateful that Solomon, the instrument God's Spirit used to pen these inspired and inerrant words, was a work in progress himself. He did not always practice what he preached, and he suffered because of his foolish decisions. But he was wise to come back to the baseline of belief in the ways of the Lord as the wisest course for living. You and I will stumble along the way with unwise actions, but wise are we to recalibrate for Christ.

Are you looking to love the Lord and people with authentic actions? Do you want to be a leader worth following, a father who is admired, a mother who is appreciated, a child who is pleasant, and a disciple of Jesus who is growing in grace? If so, then seek to know God's heart on how to live life, which He beautifully lays out in the principles of Proverbs.

Proverbs is not a magic wand that works out everything we encounter in life, but it is a guide to go with our prayers and experiences. Like a Sherpa, follow Jesus as He reveals His ways in these wise and ancient words that have proven true for over three thousand years. Wisdom has a track record of trust in God, love for God, and fear of God. Be wise!

TITLE INDEX

TITLE INDEX

TITLE INDEX

I

KEEP LEARNING

Let the wise listen and add to their learning,
and let the discerning get guidance.
Proverbs 1:5

Wise men and women are lifetime learners. The knowledge and understanding that served us well last year will not be sufficient for following years. It is what we are learning today that prepares us for tomorrow. Wisdom and discernment listen and learn. They listen to people around them and learn what to do and what not to do. Another person's unfortunate tragedy can be a teacher of decisions to avoid.

When you see the use of irresponsible debt destroy a family, you learn the discipline of saving. Another person's triumph can be a teacher of choices to embrace. The sacrifice of a mom who stays home to serve her family increases the probability of children with character. You listen and learn from her how to teach little ones to love Jesus; so keep learning.

"Instruct the wise and they will be wiser still; teach the righteous and they will add to their learning" (Proverbs 9:9).

Your counsel increases in value as you grow in wisdom and discernment. Lazy learners are left to be by themselves. It is an educated life that others desire learning; so seek out a mentor who models learning, with whom you can meet weekly to challenge your assumptions. Invite your mentor to question your answers more than answer your questions. Oral learning through the exchange of ideas unlocks and applies wisdom. You are positioned to learn in an audience of one with graying hair.

Above all, learn by submission to God and His Word. A humble life can be trusted with God's wisdom and the Holy Spirit's discernment. It is out of your compassion and mercy that knowledge is converted to wisdom. Keep learning, and the Lord will lift you to new levels of influence. Stop learning, and you will lower into irrelevance. Learning expands your kingdom effectiveness and deepens your character.

"Instruct a wise man and he will be wiser still; teach a righteous man and he will add to his learning" (Proverbs 9:9).

What lesson do I need to learn today so I can better serve the Lord and - others tomorrow?

Related Readings: Deuteronomy 5:1; 31:13; Job 34:2–4; Psalm 119:73; Hebrews 5:8

REFLECTIONS

_____

_____

_____

_____

_____

2

LISTEN TO PARENTS

Listen, my son, to your father's instruction and do not forsake
your mother's teaching.
Proverbs 1:8

Parents are God's provision for protection and learning; therefore, as we listen to them, we learn from them. We learn lessons on living frugally, being honest, and working hard. We also learn what not to do, like eating poorly, not exercising, and not forgiving. Parents teach, and children learn, whether either recognizes the educational exchange. This learning process is meant to make each generation better in the eyes of God.

Indeed, parental honor is the cornerstone of any family forged by faith in Christ. Without learning from your parents' mistakes and building on their successes, you are destined to dysfunction. You honor your parents when you listen to, learn from, and obey them. You honor God as you honor your mom and dad; so value your parents because of their position, not their performance.

"Children, obey your parents in the Lord, for this is right. 'Honor your father and mother'—which is the first commandment with a promise—'so that it may go well with you and that you may enjoy long life on the earth'" (Ephesians 6:1–3).

This high honor and esteem of parents is what keeps entire nations of families focused on what makes a lasting legacy. Once society sequesters the elderly in isolation as a burden and offers euthanasia as an option, the beginning of the end of that foolish culture has arrived. It is in our service to them that we see Jesus. Parents have the potential to provide perspective only experience affords.

Take the time to look past the rough exterior of your dad, and determine to draw out his nuggets of wisdom. Help your mom process her fears and forgive her shortcomings, and you will see the beauty of her advice. Parents are not perfect, but even in their imperfection they invite honor and attention; so listen and learn from your parents. You will learn from the Lord in the process. Parents are a gift from God; so receive them by faith, and steward the relationship in humility and love.

"You know the commandments: 'Do not commit adultery, do not murder, do not steal, do not give false testimony, honor your father and mother'" (Luke 18:20).

What area of my life will I invite my parents' advice and feedback in an honorable way?

Related Readings: Genesis 49:2; Exodus 18:24; Proverbs 23:22; 1 Timothy 5:4

REFLECTIONS

_____

_____

_____

_____

_____

3

STAND ALONE

My son, do not go along with them, do not set foot on their paths;
for their feet rush into sin, they are swift to shed blood.
Proverbs 1:15–16

Stand alone against the shameful ways of sinful men and women.
Perhaps you feel alone because no one else seems to speak up, but your
Savior stands with you in your seclusion. It is more convenient to compromise
your convictions; however, stay strong in what God says, and obey. It may be
for a season that you stand alone because your perseverance in doing what is
right will prod others to do right.

For example, avoid the bar and unseemly clubs on business trips, and others
will find the courage to join you. At college pray instead of party, study instead
of steal, serve instead of acting silly, and be faithful instead of foolish. Young
adults are longing for a reliable friend whom they can trust, from whom they
can learn, and with whom they can be in a community of accountability. Stand
alone, and see God work wonders.

"But if I do judge, my decisions are true, because I am not alone. I stand with
the Father, who sent me" (John 8:16).

It is foolish to step into a seductive snare of sin. When you see it coming, do
not go there, or you will be like a silly bird whose curiosity leads it into a trap,
loss of freedom, and death. The pain of not standing alone is reason enough
to remain in the character of Christ. However, there are other benefits. You
stand alone so yours is a compelling story of courage you can communicate to
your children now and as they grow older. You stand alone so you can look your
spouse in the eyes and honestly say you value him or her much more than
worldly whims that bring dishonor. You stand alone so the people you serve
grow in confidence that you have their very best interest in mind. Most

importantly, you stand alone by the grace of God in humility and faith.

Do not become proud of standing alone, or you will fall, suddenly and severely. You stand alone by staying on your knees in desperate dependence on God. Give Him the glory, and He will give you the gumption to go it alone when necessary.

"He whose walk is blameless and who does what is righteous, who speaks the truth from his heart...He who does these things will never be shaken" (Psalm 15:2, 5).

Where do I need to stand alone as an encouragement to those who may be holding back for fear of what others might think or do?

Related Readings: Job 23:13; Proverbs 12:7; Luke 21:19; 1 Corinthians 10:12

REFLECTIONS

_____

_____

_____

_____

_____

4

WINDOW OF OPPORTUNITY

"Since you ignored all my advice and would not accept my rebuke,
I in turn will laugh at your disaster; I will mock
when calamity overtakes you."
Proverbs 1:25–26

Windows of opportunity are finite, and before long they are gone. It may be a pending deal at work that requires you to negotiate; so do not allow greed to abort a closing. You may have a brief time to woo your woman back into a healthy home, but it requires humility and forgiveness from you as a servant leader. Or this may be a season for you to sit at the feet of a seasoned servant of the Lord.

His or her availability will soon pass, and you will be the one to whom others look for answers. God opens windows of opportunity for you to prayerfully move forward in faith. The Lord's clear glass of possibilities allows you to view vistas of His faithfulness and grace that become companions on your next great adventure in following Jesus. Windows of faith are passages into God's purpose for you.

"There is a time for everything, and a season for every activity under the heavens" (Ecclesiastes 3:1).

However, those who ridicule a relationship with Christ will look ridiculous to Him and His followers. Calamity crushes those without Christ and causes them to look foolish as they flail away without faith and hope. There is a time after death that the window to knowing God is shut. The last judgment is the Lord's opportunity to ask, "What did you do with my Son Jesus?"

At this point it is too late for a faithless life because that person has the misfortune of spending eternity in hell without God. This is why Christians labor in this life to love people to the Lord. Their window of faith will soon be shut, but in the meantime you can show them your Savior Jesus with your words and deeds. Pray for the relational windows around you to be open and won for Christ.

"The fruit of the righteous is a tree of life, and he who wins souls is wise" (Proverbs 11:30).

What current opportunities from the Lord do I need to immediately pursue by faith?

Related Readings: Deuteronomy 1:8; Judges 9:33; Luke 14:17; Acts 3:11

REFLECTIONS

_____

_____

_____

_____

_____

5

COMPLACENCY KILLS

"For the waywardness of the simple will kill them, and the complacency
of fools will destroy them, but whoever listens to me will live in safety
and be at ease, without fear of harm."
Proverbs 1:32–33

Complacency is a killer because it does not care. It kills outcomes because it does not care about excellent execution. It kills relationships because it does not care about investing in the good of another. It kills finances because it does not care if spending drifts into irresponsible expenditures. It kills life because it does not care if lethargic living leads to premature death.

However, Christ-centered living kills complacency because Jesus is full of life, opportunity, and possibilities. Christians are called to initiate and engage in intimacy with the Almighty. There is a divine drive and determination to do good for God. Complacency kills, but Christ gives life and safety without fear of harm.

"On that day messengers will go out from me in ships to frighten Cush out of her complacency. Anguish will take hold of them on the day of Egypt's doom, for it is sure to come" (Ezekiel 30:9).

You may find yourself in a funk, captured by frail faith, unable to move forward even moderately. You may be asking, "Is it even worth another try?" And the answer is, "Yes, get up and get going with God!" Kill complacency by courting Christ and His agenda for your life. The Lord cares about where you are going and how you will get there. Do not be overwhelmed by a mountain of unanswered questions. Just take the first step of faith with your heavenly Father.

Complacency and Christ cannot coexist. Your Savior will safely guide you to your next goal. Pity parties are for the complacent. Celebratory parties are for those compelled by Christ. The wise run to serve the Lord, while fools rush in to sit and soak. Through trust in Jesus, become a complacency killer, as hope takes no prisoners of pity.

"At that time I will search Jerusalem with lamps and punish those who are complacent, who are like wine left on its dregs, who think, 'The LORD will do nothing, either good or bad'" (Zephaniah 1:12).

Where do I need to remove complacency in my life and replace it with faith in Christ?

Related Readings: Amos 6:1; Psalm 14:2; 2 Thessalonians 1:3; 2 Peter 3:18

REFLECTIONS

_____

_____

_____

_____

_____

6

KNOWLEDGE OF GOD

If you look for it as for silver and search for it as for hidden treasure,
then you will understand the fear of the LORD
and find the knowledge of God.
Proverbs 2:4–5

The knowledge of God is obtained by the wisdom of God, and the wisdom of God is found in the Word of God. Jesus is the Word; so when we see Him, we not only see our Savior but our God. Jesus became flesh and walked among us so He could, among other things, teach us the knowledge of God. So read the red letters in the gospels of Christ. You will observe the knowledge of God lived out in your Lord.

You will learn obedience by understanding and applying His teachings. Obtaining the knowledge of God and integrating it into life transformation are not passive exercises. They come from passionate prayer, earnestly seeking to understand the words written in red. Knowledge of God is food that satisfies the soul. It is a divine diet of grace and truth.

"Like newborn babies, long for the pure milk of the word, so that by it you may grow in respect to salvation" (1 Peter 2:2 NASB).

You read and receive the Word of God so you can be transformed by the knowledge of God. Wisdom is the way to knowing God. It is discovered through toil and trust, industry and intimacy, hard work and heaven's illumination. Like the precious metals of silver and gold, the knowledge of God is found in the discipline and determination of digging out truth that may be covered over by the dirt of unbelief.

You rise up early so you can meditate in the mine shaft with your Master Jesus, and He shows you the way. As you humbly receive the knowledge of God, make known to others the richness of your discovery. Invest wisdom in others for the sake of God's kingdom. Perhaps you start by being the spiritual leader at work and home.

"Then on the second day the heads of fathers' households of all the people, the priests and the Levites were gathered to Ezra the scribe that they might gain insight into the words of the law" (Nehemiah 8:13 NASB).

How can I use my knowledge of God to bless and encourage others?

Related Readings: Job 28:12, 20, 23; John 1:1–14; 2 Peter 1:5

REFLECTIONS

7

DISCRETION'S PROTECTION

Discretion will protect you, and understanding will guard you.
Proverbs 2:11

Discretion arms us against evil and all matters of temptation. It is a God-inspired ability to choose wisely between good and bad, between better and best. Leaders may recognize this trait in you as they did in Joseph: "Since God has informed you of all this, there is no one so discerning and wise as you are" (Genesis 41:39 NASB). So stay humble if heaven has graced you with insight into what needs to be done.

Others are more apt to receive your instruction if it is delivered in a trustworthy tone and with a humble spirit. Do not allow your overconfidence to forget Christ and fuel jealousy in the insecure. Use your discretion for the good of the entire enterprise. It is meant to be used as a protector and not as a pass for pride to wreak havoc. Discretion is a sentinel for your soul's care and welfare.

"My son, do not let wisdom and understanding out of your sight, preserve sound judgment and discretion" (Proverbs 3:21).

Furthermore, use discretion with sensitive information. Your position of influence is to protect innocent parties, not cause unnecessary chaos. For example, instead of embarrassing others in front of the group for their incompetency, talk with them alone in a spirit of collaborative correction. You can protect the reputation of a team member and still experience excellent outcome within the organization.

Make sure to move discretion from your head to your heart so insight is communicated with grace and clarity. Ultimately, it is God's discretion as it relates to opportunities and results. Thus, seek His face by faith to learn how to protect and progress in His will.

"For his God instructs and teaches him properly" (Isaiah 28:26 NASB).

What pressing family issue needs my discretion and protection from foolishness?

Related Readings: Nehemiah 8:12; Ecclesiastes 9:15–18; Ephesians 5:15

REFLECTIONS

8

MARRIAGE COVENANT

It [wisdom] will save you also from the adulteress, from the wayward
wife with her seductive words, who has left the partner of her youth
and ignored the covenant she made before God.
Proverbs 2:16–17

Marriage is a covenant before God, not to be messed with by man.
It is not a secular ceremony but a Christ-centered commitment "until death do
us part." However, there are tempters, both men and women, who try to take
away the trust between a husband and wife. Their lives are unhappy; so they
scheme for artificial satisfaction at the expense of someone else's marriage.

Sin is not passive but active; so be on prayerful alert not to listen to its allure.
Pay attention, and do not place yourself in compromising circumstances.
Marriage is a sacred obligation. God is not only a witness but the party having
instituted the ordinance; so stay true to Him and your true love.

"Marriage should be honored by all, and the marriage bed kept pure, for God
will judge the adulterer and all the sexually immoral" (Hebrews 13:4).

Marriage is accountability between husband and wife under the authority of
almighty God. This is why wayward men and women do not get away with
disrespecting marriage vows. Disobedience to an oath before God leads to the
damage and even death of relationships, reputation, financial security,
emotional stability, and physical health. Husbands and wives who seriously take
their commitment to Christ and each other are not seduced into sex outside
their marriage.

How do you maintain this high standard of honor? By God's grace you romance
each other like the days when you were dating. You share your heart and
affections only with your true love, the bride of your youth. You determine not to
be alone with anyone of the opposite sex, as this can feed temptation. Lastly,

celebrate and uphold marriage as a solemn covenant before the Lord, family, friends, and each other.

"Therefore, thus says the Lord GOD, 'As I live, surely My oath which he despised and My covenant which he broke, I will inflict on his head'" (Ezekiel 17:19 NASB).

How can I honor my spouse by respecting our marriage as a covenant before God?

Related Readings: Numbers 5:12–22; Malachi 2:14–16; Matthew 5:27–32

☙

REFLECTIONS

_____

_____

_____

_____

_____

9

WALKING WISELY

Thus you will walk in the ways of good men and keep
to the paths of the righteous.
Proverbs 2:20

Walking wisely means you keep company with those who love and obey Christ. They are your influencers because their values reflect the route you want to take in life. There is an alignment of purpose with people who pray together on behalf of the greater good of God's kingdom. So in college, walk with the crowd who is all about character building, service to others, studies, love for the Lord, and obedience to His commands.

At work, prayerfully partner with those who are principled in their business philosophy. Others may have less skill and experience, but you can trust their heart to do what they say they will do. Moreover, do not negotiate with mediocre living as it is distasteful in the mouth of your Master Jesus. Instead, walk with those who raise you to righteous living.

"Walk with the wise and become wise, for a companion of fools suffers harm" (Proverbs 13:20).

Of course, you are to reach out and care for sinners with the purpose of loving them to the Lord. God has placed you in the life of unbelievers to influence them toward heaven. Perhaps one day they will thank you for your patience and prayers. Walking wisely means you learn well by being with those who aspire for intimacy with the Almighty. You walk with the ones who obey the One.

Furthermore, your family may need you to slow down because you have run so far ahead they are unable to keep up and benefit from your presence. Walk with your sons and daughters while you can. Your leadership at work will advance in significance when your team walks with you in focus. Above all else, walk with the Lord, and He will give you wisdom and insight into whom to walk with and where.

"This is what the LORD says: 'Stand at the crossroads and look; ask for the ancient paths, ask where the good way is, and walk in it, and you will find rest for your souls. But you said, "We will not walk in it"'" (Jeremiah 6:16).

With whom do I need to cease walking, with whom do I need to continue walking, and with whom do I need to begin walking?

Related Readings: Psalm 119:63–115; 1 Corinthians 5:11; Hebrews 6:12

REFLECTIONS

_____

_____

_____

_____

_____

HUMBLE WISDOM

Do not be wise in your own eyes; fear the LORD and shun evil.
Proverbs 3:7

Humble wisdom does not hint at a holier-than-thou attitude. On the contrary, it is contrite before Christ and modest before men. Humble wisdom is very grateful to God for His blessing of insight and understanding into eternal matters. Wisdom is not a badge of superiority to be worn with pride, but a blanket of security that humbles the heart.

Wisdom without humility becomes conceited and is accompanied by a condescending attitude. It is ugly as it disfigures the soul. It is like star athletes who are so full of themselves they fail to reach their potential for lack of team support. However, humble wisdom says, "I am a fellow learner of the Lord's ways; I am a work in progress just like you." It is to a heart of humility that God entrusts His wisdom; so stay desperate for divine direction.

"Who is wise and understanding among you? Let them show it by their good life, by deeds done in the humility that comes from wisdom" (James 3:13).

The more wisdom increases in your heart and mind, the more pride needs to decrease in your persona. It is the fear of the Lord that keeps you from thinking you can be anything special outside of your Savior Jesus. The fear of God does not forget that wisdom comes from above. Yes, your experience enhances wisdom, and your pain can produce wisdom, but ultimately wisdom resides with God and His Word.

This is why in humility you hunker down and pray:

Heavenly Father, I bow in awe before you and ask for insight and direction. You are the author of all wisdom.

It is submission to Christ and His command that squeezes out selfish, worldly wisdom and replaces it with the humble wisdom of heaven. Therefore, request wisdom for His glory, and never cease to learn from those whom the Lord sends daily into your life.

"Live in harmony with one another; do not be haughty (snobbish, high-minded, exclusive), but readily adjust yourself to [people, things] and give yourselves to humble tasks. Never overestimate yourself or be wise in your own conceits" (Romans 12:16 AB).

Whom can I learn from today to become wiser in humility of mind and heart?

Related Readings: 1 Kings 3:4–15; Isaiah 5:21; Romans 11:20–25; Revelation 14:7

REFLECTIONS

_____

_____

_____

_____

_____

11

HONORABLE WEALTH

Honor the LORD with your wealth, with the firstfruits
of all your crops; then your barns will be filled to overflowing,
and your vats will brim over with new wine.
Proverbs 3:9–10

Why do we honor the Lord with our wealth? We honor Him because He is the giver of all good things, the author of our abundance. As our estate grows, so should our honor of our heavenly Father. Otherwise, we are tempted to take credit for our success, honoring ourselves. The Bible says, "You may say in your heart, 'My power and the strength of my hand made me this wealth'" (Deuteronomy 8:17 NASB).

In some seasons our net worth decreases, and we are reminded that Christ controls cash flow. Wealth is not an end to itself but the means to the greater goal of honoring God. Peace and contentment flow from wealth that honors the Lord, while fear and insecurity consume the heart that honors itself. The Bible says, "If riches increase, do not set your heart upon them" (Psalm 62:10 NASB).

So how do you honor the Lord with your wealth? One way is to remain faithful and give Him the firstfruits of your fortune. Small or large as it may be, His primary concern is your faithfulness to give. You give out of obedience, not abundance. People see Christ when you keep your cash commitments, especially when it costs you. This is honorable in heaven and on earth. Give to your church, the poor and needy, widows, orphans, family, and ministries who align with your passions.

The result of your generous giving in the middle of downward financial pressure will be an upward blessing to you and the recipients. Your honorable use of wealth for Jesus' sake may mean food, clothing, shelter, and medical supplies for a village, or Bibles translated into the foreign tongue of a remote people halfway around the world. The best time to aggressively give is when the need is greatest. You take care of honoring Christ with generous giving, and He will take care of you. What you give now, you will have in abundance later.

"And you will be blessed, since they do not have the means to repay you; for you will be repaid at the resurrection of the righteous" (Luke 14:14 NASB).

How can I be honorable and remain faithful to my financial commitments to Christ?

Related Readings: Deuteronomy 26:2–15; Luke 12:18–24; 1 Corinthians 15:20; Philippians 4:17–18

REFLECTIONS

_____

_____

_____

_____

_____

12

SOUND JUDGMENT

My son, preserve sound judgment and discernment, do not let them
out of your sight; they will be life for you, an ornament to grace your neck.
Proverbs 3:21–22

Sound judgment leads to the best decisions, which lead to wise living. It is sound judgment that keeps you from being sucked into the schemes of fools. It is sound judgment that resists spending all now so you can save for the future. It is sound judgment that does not run ahead of God but trusts His timing at work and home.

Sound judgment plans a wise sequence of steps before it invests time and money. We get into trouble when we forget to do what we set out to do in the first place. I often ask myself, "Have my motives drifted from their original intent to glorify God?" If not careful, instead of preserving sound judgment, I allow it to expire for lack of attention.

"These are the things you are to do: Speak the truth to each other, and render true and sound judgment in your courts" (Zechariah 8:16).

Therefore, stay focused with both eyes fixed on your heavenly Father's eternal wisdom. Do not allow one lazy eye to drift toward the expedient way of the world. It is the Holy Spirit's discernment within you that keeps you riveted on the truth. So regularly romance God's Word, and your affections will remain keenly aware of the Almighty's agenda. Life for your soul is the fruit of wise focus.

The Holy Spirit gives you the inner energy and discernment to execute His plan. For example, as you prepare, listen intently to the voices clamoring for your attention, and weed out the ones void of humility. Lastly, His grace adorns the actions of those who walk in wisdom and sound judgment. Graciousness governs wise behavior. So seek the Lord for discernment and insight. Wait on

God, for sound judgment rests in a wise and discerning heart.

"I am your servant; give me discernment that I may understand your statutes" (Psalm 119:125).

Where do I need to be patient, waiting on the Holy Spirit's discernment, so I can wisely apply sound judgment?

Related Readings: Job 28:12–28; Joshua 1:8; John 15:6–7; Hebrews 2:1–3

REFLECTIONS

_____

_____

_____

_____

_____

13

SWEET SLEEP

When you lie down, you will not be afraid; when you lie down,
your sleep will be sweet.
Proverbs 3:24

Sweet sleep comes to a secure soul. Wise is the one who lays his worries at the feet of Jesus before he lies down at night. Fear is foreign to those who sleep sweetly in the safe arms of their Savior. If you are a light sleeper, learn to listen to the Lord, write down what He is saying, and go back to bed. The Almighty may awaken you, as He did Samuel (see 1 Samuel 3), only to rock you back to sleep in a more restful place.

The Lord neither sleeps nor slumbers, as He is a trustworthy sentinel over the vulnerable state of your blissful exposure. God is on guard; so you do not have to sit up and see what is going on. You can lie down by faith and wake up rested and refreshed. A good night's rest is a gift from God, ready to be received by faith. David, a man who faced many fears, confidently prayed:

"In peace I will both lie down and sleep, for You alone, O LORD, make me to dwell in safety" (Psalm 4:8 NASB).

Furthermore, a clear conscience is what Christ uses to calm your emotions, settle your mind, and create sweet sleep. When demons of guilt are engaged in your head, you have a hard time sleeping. However, a clear conscience comes by humbly taking responsibility for your behavior and asking forgiveness from God and man for sinful attitudes and actions. Integrity and uprightness preserve you from pride and precarious living.

A clear conscience results from working through relational conflict. Why allow broken relationships to rob you of rest? Instead, go immediately in humility, and initiate reconciliation that will lead to rest, as stress surrenders at the sight of relational healing. Simply talking through tension with a teachable heart releases anxieties and fears. A clear conscience that keeps short accounts will benefit in sweet sleep.

"Therefore, if you are offering your gift at the altar and there remember that your brother has something against you, leave your gift there in front of the altar. First go and be reconciled to your brother; then come and offer your gift" (Matthew 5:23–24).

With whom do I need to seek reconciliation so we can both rest in sweet sleep?

Related Readings: Job 11:18; Psalm 121:4–7; Mark 4:38; Acts 12:6

REFLECTIONS

14

GOD BLESSED HOME

*The LORD'S curse is on the house of the wicked,
but he blesses the home of the righteous.
Proverbs 3:33*

What type of home does the Lord bless? He blesses a home that trusts Him and does what is right, as God defines right. A home that prioritizes the implementation of heaven's agenda on earth, He blesses. A home that builds up rather than tears down, He blesses. A home that humbly reads Scripture together and seeks to personally apply its truth, He blesses. A home that prays together, plays together, worships together, and serves together, He blesses.

"God bless our home" is a wise prayer for a family of faith. Even if your home is more like hell than heaven, you can still make a significant difference. Let your light of love shine in service to undeserving family members, and your heavenly Father will draw them unto Himself. God blesses a home shingled with unselfish service.

"But if serving the LORD seems undesirable to you, then choose for yourselves this day whom you will serve, whether the gods your ancestors served beyond the Euphrates, or the gods of the Amorites, in whose land you are living. But as for me and my household, we will serve the LORD" (Joshua 24:15).

You may be the spiritual leader of the home, but you do not have the confidence to lead in religious matters. There is hope. First of all, keep it simple by spending time alone with the Lord. Take what He is teaching you in His Word, and transfer it to your family. If you are learning humility, read a Bible verse about the humble, and share a recent humbling experience from your life.

God blesses a leader in the home who is authentic and transparent. Family members can relate to your real struggles instead of perceived perfection. The home is heaven's hospital for healing, encouragement, and accountability. Make Christianity work at home; then you have the creditability of a God-blessed model to export into the church and community. Christ shows contempt for the house of sinners but blesses the home of wise saints.

"By wisdom a house is built, and through understanding it is established" (Proverbs 24:3).

By God's grace, how can I make our home a haven of rest and righteous behavior?

Related Readings: Deuteronomy 28:2–68; Malachi 2:2; Matthew 12:43–45; Acts 16:29–34

☙

REFLECTIONS

_____

_____

_____

_____

_____

15

LISTEN TO DAD

Listen, my sons, to a father's instruction; pay attention
and gain understanding.
Proverbs 4:1

**We dads do not always get it right, but on occasion we do have
something outstanding to say.** Because dads have a divine directive to
parent their children, they deserve an audience. Even if your dad is not a
Christian (or of lesser character), respect his role, and listen to his instruction.
Your dad is an avenue of discovery for wisdom and insight.

If your dad is distant and disinterested, take the time to reach out and build up
the brittle relationship. Dads desire and deserve honor, and your love is a light
into their lives. If your dad is deceased or nowhere to be found, find a father
figure from whom you can learn. Pray for a person whose perspective is shaped
by Scripture, who can show you the way to live by his attitudes and actions.
Above all, be with your dad so you can hear and learn from him.

"And you shall teach them to your sons, talking of them when you sit in your
house and when you walk along the road and when you lie down and when you
rise up" (Deuteronomy 11:19 NASB).

As a dad, be available, approachable, and accountable to engage your children
in educational environments. They need to know why diligence in their studies
is important; it prepares the mind for relational maturity and successful work.
They need to know why it is wise to save their emotional and physical intimacy
for their husband or wife; it makes for a much-healthier marriage, and it is a
mandate from God. They need to know how to save, spend, and share money
so they can become responsible money managers, not remaining codependent
on you beyond college.

A dad's work begins when he leaves his job at 5:00 P.M. to go home. At home is your opportunity to encourage and instruct your children in the ways of the Lord. Read a chapter of Proverbs over dinner, wash the car together, or take a walk in the park. You are the headmaster of your home; so instruct with grace and truth.

"Just as you know how we were exhorting and encouraging and imploring each one of you as a father would his own children, so that you may walk in a manner worthy of the God who calls you into His own kingdom and glory" (1 Thessalonians 2:11–12 NASB).

When can I set a time (sooner than later) to be with my dad and/or children for instruction and learning?

Related Readings: Deuteronomy 4:9; Job 33:33; Psalm 32:8; Hebrews 2:1

REFLECTIONS

16

LONG LIFE

Listen, my son, accept what I say, and the years of your life will be many.
Proverbs 4:10

Long life is not guaranteed for anyone because we have no promise of tomorrow. Each day is a gift from God. However, as a whole, pure living can prolong life. Accidents and unfortunate illnesses can strike suddenly and snatch life from a vibrant soul, but wise living is still a road to long life. A fool eats, drinks, and is merry as if there is no tomorrow, while wisdom plans and prepares for the return of Christ at any moment.

Wisdom focuses on godly living, while godless living is the focus of fools. It may seem like the disobedient are getting away with something, as some frolic into their frail years, but judgment is coming, not to mention the harmful consequences in this life. Therefore, listen to wisdom and obey its precepts so you are positioned to live a long, full life.

"Children, obey your parents in the Lord, for this is right. 'Honor your father and mother'—which is the first commandment with a promise—'so that it may go well with you and that you may enjoy long life on the earth'" (Ephesians 6:1–3).

Furthermore, romance wisdom with your emotions and affections. True lovers of wisdom embrace and exalt the beauty she brings to a life. You are attractive when you choose to live wisely under the authority of almighty God. Your family, friends, and work associates are drawn to your wise decisions saturated in prayer, collaborated with experts, and based on the principles of God's Word.

Concur with Christ on the truth of His Word, and He will bless you. Wisdom is the primary principle because it puts you on the path of life. Therefore, follow the Lord. In His infinite wisdom, He will direct your steps and determine your length of days on earth with eternal life to come. Obedience of Christ's commands leads you into wise living that is truly life.

"And He said to him, 'Why are you asking Me about what is good? There is only One who is good; but if you wish to enter into life, keep the commandments'" (Matthew 19:17 NASB).

Where can I find and receive wisdom for the glory of God?

Related Readings: Psalm 119:9; Luke 12:18–20; 1 Thessalonians 2:13; James 4:14

REFLECTIONS

_____

_____

_____

_____

_____

17

WISE GUIDES

I guide you in the way of wisdom and lead you along straight paths.
Proverbs 4:11

God places wise guides in our life to lead us in the way of wisdom.
These are men and women with a touch of gray or a hoary head full of fine silver and discernment. Their counsel is the cream that rises to the top from all the advice we receive. We value their opinions as a righteous road map from our heavenly Father. Perhaps you meet an hour or two weekly with these sages from your Savior so you can better see the wise way to walk.

Life is full of circumstances that make your path crooked, but you can stay focused on the way of wisdom through wise guides and aggressive prayer. Ask prayer from fellow wisdom hunters for your heart to traffic on the path of purity. The righteous prayers of wisdom reveal the way with heaven's headlights; so request prayer often.

"This is what the LORD says: 'Stand at the crossroads and look; ask for the ancient paths, ask where the good way is, and walk in it, and you will find rest for your souls. But you said, "We will not walk in it"'" (Jeremiah 6:16).

Solicit the prayers of wise saints who seek the Lord daily in determined intercession. Ask them to pray for your heart, mind, and body to be kept clean in Christ Jesus. Entrust wise prayer warriors with specific financial and family issues that need a touch from heaven. It is not only okay but also necessary for a prayer team to surround you as ambassadors to almighty God on your behalf.

They convoy with you and Christ to make the crooked ways straight. Wise guides pray that your trust is in Christ, the conductor of your life and work. So, sooner than later, prayerfully invite wise guides, passionate about prayer, who will go to

God on your behalf. Then as you debrief together on what He is doing, your intimacy with the Lord and each other will grow, and your understanding of the wisest way to go will be marked more clearly.

"Make me know Thy ways, O LORD; Teach me Thy paths. Lead me in Thy truth and teach me, For Thou art the God of my salvation; For Thee I wait all the day" (Psalm 25:4–5 NASB).

Whom can I ask to be a wise guide in my life? Who will pray I walk in wisdom and on the path of Christ?

Related Readings: 1 Samuel 12:23–24; Isaiah 2:3; Acts 13:9–10; Hebrews 12:11–13

REFLECTIONS

_____

_____

_____

_____

_____

18

PRAYERFUL PERSEVERANCE

The path of the righteous is like the first gleam of dawn,
shining ever brighter till the full light of day.
Proverbs 4:18

Prayerful perseverance is the path of the righteous. It is the route the righteous take during recessionary times. Economic downturns can be a detour in our walk with Christ, or they can shed light on where God wants us to go. You persevere in prayer because it is here the voices of worry go mute. Here your Master guides you onto a productive path. Indeed, recessions force us to be resourceful with our relationships and creativity.

Perhaps you reach out to those who have helped you in the past and are unable to help now because of their need. For example, take the time to connect those out of work with opportunities that may match their call. Most importantly, ask others how you can specifically pray for them. The Lord leads by the light of His love during dark days; so stay connected to Christ and people in prayer. This righteous resolve takes focus and hard work.

"You need to persevere so that when you have done the will of God, you will receive what he has promised" (Hebrews 10:36).

The spirit is willing, but the flesh is weak. This is why it is imperative you feed the spirit in persistent prayer. Stay engaged with God. The gleaming dawn of hope will rise on your shadowed circumstances. As you prayerfully walk with the Lord in the light, there is a holy security, a serene spirit that shines forth from your countenance for all to see. Your humble and good works on earth bring glory to your Father in heaven.

Prayerful perseverance increases the brightness of your light like the rising of the all-consuming, orange sun. So use recessionary days to heal the hurting, rescue the repentant, and comfort the broken. Dark days were created for the care of Christians to come forth in faith and generosity. Therefore, prayerfully persevere for your soul's sake, for God's glory, and in service to others.

"Then your light will break out like the dawn, And your recovery will speedily spring forth; And your righteousness will go before you; The glory of the LORD will be your rear guard" (Isaiah 58:8 NASB).

Where do I need to persevere in prayer, and whom can I specifically pray for in their dark night of the soul?

Related Readings: Job 22:28; Matthew 5:16; 26:41 KJV; Philippians 2:15

REFLECTIONS

_____

_____

_____

_____

_____

19

GUARD YOUR HEART

Above all else, guard your heart, for it is the wellspring of life.
Proverbs 4:23

Guard your heart, for it is here the Lord gives life. It is truly life because it bubbles up with tremendous trust in Him. A heart on guard for God deeply desires love for Him and obedience to His ways. There is a compelling call to follow Christ through the best and worst of circumstances. Therefore, guard your heart from disbelief so doubt does not become despair.

Guard your heart from unforgiveness so anger does not become bitterness. Guard your heart from pornography so lust does not become lasciviousness. Guard your heart from worry so fear does not become frantic. Lastly, guard your heart from pride so your attitude does not become arrogant. A guarded heart increases the probability of good things from God. A guarded inward man makes for a good outward man.

"And the peace of God, which transcends all understanding, will guard your hearts and your minds in Christ Jesus" (Philippians 4:7).

So how do you guard your heart from being defiled by sin and disturbed by trouble? One simple safeguard is using wisdom in what you watch, as your eyes encamp around your affections. Secondly, be watchful about what words enter your ears. If you listen to lies over and over again, they can easily become truth in your thinking.

Thirdly, ask God to be the guardian of where you go. Environment greatly influences the outcome of your heart. Indeed, a guarded heart is a candidate for greatness with God. Ask the Holy Spirit to hunker down in your heart and bring bold leadership to your life and swift conviction to your soul. Be on guard, and a wellspring of life will gush forth for God's glory.

"May the words of my mouth and the meditation of my heart be pleasing in your sight, O LORD, my Rock and my Redeemer" (Psalm 19:14).

Whom will I ask to hold me accountable in what I watch so my heart is clean and pure?

Related Readings: Deuteronomy 4:9; Psalm 139:23–24; Jeremiah 17:9; Mark 7:21–23

REFLECTIONS

_____

_____

_____

_____

_____

20

EMOTIONAL EMPTINESS

Above all else, guard your heart, for it is the wellspring of life.
Proverbs 4:23

Emotional emptiness is a setup for frustrated and insecure living.
If I ignore my emotional bank account with bad behavior, I can easily become overdrawn and withdraw into my silent shell. There are late fees that result in broken promises, missed appointments, and angry outbursts. Emotional emptiness easily leads to chronic exhaustion.

Bad emotions such as unresolved anger overcome those running on emotional empty. In addition, good things like serving others can suck the joy and gratitude from your life if you are not emotionally whole. Resentment runs rampant when your emotions are on the edge of emptiness; so guard your heart with the Holy Spirit's help and wisdom.

"A cheerful heart is good medicine, but a crushed spirit dries up the bones" (Proverbs 17:22).

So how do you know if you are approaching emotional emptiness? If you are emotionally spent, how do you replenish your emotional bank account? One sign of emotional fatigue is when your feelings are easily hurt. You take too much personally without appropriating forgiveness and trust in the Lord's ability to handle the situation. So invite God to grow your character during challenging times.

One way to involve Jesus in your emotional barrenness is to write out your fears and talk them through with the One whom you totally trust. He will give you courage to encounter those whom you fear with humility and courage. Lastly, make regular appointments with encouragers who lift you to the Lord with their affirmation and prayers.

Look for those who remind you to place your hope in heaven. Emotional fullness is created in a prayerful pace of living. Protect your emotions; they give understanding and insight into you, others, and the Lord. Above all else, trust in the peace of God to make whole your emotions and to guard your heart.

"And the peace of God, which transcends all understanding, will guard your hearts and your minds in Christ Jesus" (Philippians 4:7).

When can I block out weekly time on my calendar to guard my heart and replenish my emotional emptiness?

Related Readings: Proverbs 15:30; 22:11; 1 Timothy 1:5; 2 Timothy 2:22

☗
REFLECTIONS

_____

_____

_____

_____

_____

21

PAY ATTENTION

My son, pay attention to my wisdom; listen well to my words of insight.
Proverbs 5:1

Pay attention to the wise and discerning around you. They have perspective that penetrates through your bias and blind spots. If you ignore their admonishments, you may miss God's best, or at worst spend a long time recovering from a raw deal. Wisdom is a watchman that keeps us from entering into unfit relationships. Beware of those who only want you for what they need, with no regard for the needs of others.

If I ignore my emotional bank account with bad behavior, I can easily become overdrawn and withdraw into my silent shell. There are late fees that result in broken promises, missed appointments, and angry outbursts. Emotional emptiness easily leads to chronic exhaustion.

Bad emotions such as unresolved anger overcome those running on emotional empty. In addition, good things like serving others can suck the joy and gratitude from your life if you are not emotionally whole. Resentment runs rampant when your emotions are on the edge of emptiness; so guard your heart with the Holy Spirit's help and wisdom.

"A cheerful heart is good medicine, but a crushed spirit dries up the bones" (Proverbs 17:22).

So how do you know if you are approaching emotional emptiness? If you are emotionally spent, how do you replenish your emotional bank account? One sign of emotional fatigue is when your feelings are easily hurt. You take too much personally without appropriating forgiveness and trust in the Lord's ability to handle the situation. So invite God to grow your character during challenging times.

One way to involve Jesus in your emotional barrenness is to write out your fears and talk them through with the One whom you totally trust. He will give you courage to encounter those whom you fear with humility and courage. Lastly, make regular appointments with encouragers who lift you to the Lord with their affirmation and prayers.

Look for those who remind you to place your hope in heaven. Emotional fullness is created in a prayerful pace of living. Protect your emotions; they give understanding and insight into you, others, and the Lord. Above all else, trust in the peace of God to make whole your emotions and to guard your heart.

"And the peace of God, which transcends all understanding, will guard your hearts and your minds in Christ Jesus" (Philippians 4:7).

When can I block out weekly time on my calendar to guard my heart and replenish my emotional emptiness?

Related Readings: Proverbs 15:30; 22:11; 1 Timothy 1:5; 2 Timothy 2:22

REFLECTIONS

_____

_____

_____

_____

_____

22

WISE HIRE

Like an archer who wounds at random
is he who hires a fool or any passer-by.
Proverbs 26:10

It is hard to hire just the right person, for the right role, at the right time. Most of the time, it is better to leave a position vacant than to fill it prematurely with the wrong person. Your hiring process needs to be rigorous so the probability of success is high. For example, be extremely cautious in hiring someone just because you are comfortable with the person or because he or she is a friend. Relationships are at risk when work is in the mix.

Familiarity can push against accountability and, if necessary, the ability to fire a friend. So take time to hire someone. Engage him or her only after prayerful, thorough due diligence and team consent. Otherwise, the opportunity for foolish behavior and wounded relationships increases. Staff suffers under the chronic failures of fools who flail away in unfocused activity.

"Do not take advantage of a hired worker who is poor and needy, whether that worker is a fellow Israelite or a foreigner residing in one of your towns" (Deuteronomy 24:14).

This is why time, talent, and testing are necessary to determine if there is alignment between the prospective employee and the organization. Temperament, skills, and emotional intelligence assessments are objective tools that give a three-dimensional perspective of the prospective team member. Someone may be a genius with spreadsheets and numbers but lack the emotional maturity to handle conflict and/or the ability to communicate well.

Training can shore up some skills and experience can educate, but raw talent and integrity are necessary for an outstanding outcome. Make sure you hire for results, but results that rise from the right reasons. Wise hires come with time. They have the character and track record of success to exceed employer expectations. Pray for people who will make their peers more productive and who will elevate excellence within the enterprise. Pray for God's hand in your hiring, and validate your intuition with a proven process of checks and balances.

"Make plans by seeking advice; if you wage war, obtain guidance" (Proverbs 20:18).

What role do I need to fill next, and who can help me define the best hiring process?

Related Readings: Exodus 18:13–27; Matthew 20:1–16; Luke 15:15–17

♛
REFLECTIONS

_____

_____

_____

_____

_____

23

DEADLY ADULTERY

Her feet go down to death; her steps lead straight to the grave.
Proverbs 5:5

Adultery is deadly. It kills relationships and destroys reputations. Children of a parent caught in adultery become confused, dismayed, and angry. A child is innocent of a parent's infidelity but still suffers the consequences of ongoing conflict, pain, and resentment. Without trust in the Lord and the transforming power of the Holy Spirit's healing and forgiveness, suffering children are set on a similar path of destruction.

Indeed, the ripple effect of adultery's actions can be felt for generations; so run from this raw deal. It is not worth breaking the heart of God and those who love you the most. Do not allow instant gratification to numb you from the devastating effect of selfish whims. What is done in the darkness will come to light, and it is detrimental. Like the insidious work of termites, integrity's foundation begins to crumble.

"He will bring to light what is hidden in darkness and will expose the motives of men's hearts" (1 Corinthians 4:5). Therefore, stay faithful to your bride or groom, and you will reap the rewards of relational life and respect from your children.

How can you be on guard against adultery's allurement? One way is to avoid websites that offer virtual temptation. We mock God when we pray, "Lead me not into temptation" (Matthew 6:13) and then expose ourselves to escapades that lead to adultery. So ask for accountability, and install software that blocks bad sites. Secondly, save emotional intimacy and time alone for your spouse only. Heart connection needs only to occur between a husband and wife. Friendly flirtation is the first step into adultery's intoxicating control; so inoculate your life from adultery's infection with a healthy marriage.

Husbands and wives who have emotional and physical fulfillment at home are not easily led astray. Moreover, make loving the Lord and obeying His commands your compelling commitment. God's discipline is sure for those who select the sinful action of adultery. Yes, He forgives, but He also disciplines those whom He loves. Therefore, remain on the high road of faith and fidelity. Avoid the death of adultery with a life-giving marriage.

"Marriage should be honored by all, and the marriage bed kept pure, for God will judge the adulterer and all the sexually immoral" (Hebrews 13:4).

Whom can I ask for accountability, specifically regarding wisdom with my time and freedom?

Related Readings: Genesis 39:7–9; Judges 16:5–15; Matthew 5:27–30; 1 Timothy 1:9–11

REFLECTIONS

_____

_____

_____

_____

_____

24

DIVIDED ASSETS

Strangers will consume your wealth,
and someone else will enjoy the fruit of your labor.
Proverbs 5:10 NLT

There are unfortunate actions that lead to the division of our assets.
One is divorce, and the other is the dissolving of a business relationship. It is a difficult process because each person involved has a perspective of what he or she wants. Money and stuff have a way of dividing loyalties and making friends enemies. Emotional trauma can take over and cause all parties to speak solely through their legal counsel.

It is a crime in heaven when Christians cannot work things out on earth without relying on the world's legal system. Furthermore, do not underestimate the financial free-for-all that can occur as the result of divorce or the breaking of any vow or contract. Christ commands relational commitment because it promotes financial oneness and wholeness. Otherwise, a life without direction or conviction tends to move toward financial conflict.

"Jesus continued: 'There was a man who had two sons. The younger one said to his father, "Father, give me my share of the estate." So he divided his property between them'" (Luke 15:11–12).

How will you respond when someone else, even a stranger, spends your hard-earned money? One remedy to remorse of riches is to remain a steward of God's stuff. The division of wealth is the distribution of the Almighty's assets. You are your Master's money manager. Let go of having to control the cash, and Christ's peace and contentment will control you. Allow the division of assets to humble you, bringing you to a place of brokenness, so you can better serve the Lord and people. Above all else, stay true to your marriage covenant. As a couple, you can grow God's assets for His glory.

"You cry out, 'Why doesn't the LORD accept my worship?' I'll tell you why! Because the LORD witnessed the vows you and your wife made when you were young. But you have been unfaithful to her, though she remained your faithful partner, the wife of your marriage vows. Didn't the LORD make you one with your wife? In body and spirit you are his. And what does he want? Godly children from your union. So guard your heart; remain loyal to the wife of your youth" (Malachi 2:14–15 NLT).

How can I remain faithful, avoiding the destruction of divorce and the upheaval of a financial breakup?

Related Readings: 1 Kings 11:1; Psalm 119:9; Proverbs 2:16–18; Luke 15:30

♕

REFLECTIONS

_____

_____

_____

_____

_____

25

MIDLIFE CRISIS

May your fountain be blessed, and may you rejoice in the wife
of your youth. A loving doe, a graceful deer—may her breasts
satisfy you always, may you ever be captivated by her love.
Proverbs 5:18–19

A midlife crisis means you are most likely discontent. You may be discontent with your wife, your work, and your car. However, the Bible is very clear about being content with what or with whom God has blessed you, especially your spouse. His desire is for you to want what you have and not obsess over what you do not have. Remember the bride of your youth. Celebrate her coming-out party.

Perhaps you married her because she was cute and cuddly, she cared about you, and she loved Christ. Those are compelling characteristics that hopefully have grown over the years. Be joyful in Jesus and grateful to God that He has given you a woman who walks with Him and wants to be with you. Rejoice in the wife of your youth as she keeps you young and yearning for Yahweh.

"I am not saying this because I am in need, for I have learned to be content whatever the circumstances" (Philippians 4:11).

Moreover, be captivated by the love of your wife. Her capacity and willingness to love you will grow as you consistently and unconditionally love her. What wife will not embrace her husband who serves her like his Savior Jesus serves? Love and respect create love and respect. It is a Christlike cycle. Be captivated by the love of your wife, knowing she was given to you by God. You chose her; so be pleased with your choice. In His providence He pronounced you husband and wife.

Lastly, a wife captivates her husband with her kind character and attractive looks. You wooed the husband of your youth by your sweet spirit, your delightful smell, and your inviting beauty. Be very intentional to make your love interesting to your husband who may be easily bored in the bedroom. Let the distractions of life and the activities of raising children rank second to your captivating love for each other. The will of God is to stay faithful as husband and wife. This is the true goal for marriages that stay together.

"And as the bridegroom rejoices over the bride, So your God will rejoice over you" (Isaiah 62:5 NASB).

How can I love my wife in a way that brings alive her captivating love?

Related Readings: Song of Songs 4:5; Ecclesiastes 9:9; 1 Corinthians 7:2; Ephesians 5:28

REFLECTIONS

_____

_____

_____

_____

_____

26

ETERNAL EXAMINATION

For a man's ways are in full view of the LORD,
and he examines all his paths.
Proverbs 5:21

There is an eternal eye that watches our every move. Almighty God does not exhaust from examination because He knows we need the accountability of His watchful eye. We do better when we know Deity is watching. This is why you train your children to be accountable to God. When they move out and move on, they fear God and are motivated to love and obey Him. You cannot follow your teenagers and young adult children everywhere, but the Lord does.

This is how the Holy Spirit is able to check a woman's conscience or prick a man's pride. Every good or bad deed is in full view of your heavenly Father for your benefit. He sees what a situation will bring and seeks to guide you in the right direction. This is why prayer is imperative to gain God's perspective. An eternally examined life is a gateway to knowing God. Live your life ever mindful that you are under your Master's microscope of concern, and you are freed by faith in Him.

"For God will bring every act to judgment, everything which is hidden, whether it is good or evil" (Ecclesiastes 12:14 NASB).

God's accountability is not bondage but freedom. You live within God's guidelines but with tremendous freedom and creativity on the playing field of Providence. It is those who stray into sin who are snared by its seduction. There are no secrets with your Savior, as every action will be weighed and brought into judgment.

Therefore, come clean with Christ in confession, claiming a clear conscious.

Do not let pride keep you from pronouncing your blind spots to friends who will lovingly and boldly bring them to your attention. There is no such thing as an unexamined life, as the Lord is looking. Behave in a way that makes Him smile as He gazes on your life with humble holiness. Indeed, the Lord looks on for your blessing and benefit.

"And there is no creature hidden from His sight, but all things are open and laid bare to the eyes of Him with whom we have to do" (Hebrews 4:13 NASB).

Which of my blind spots do I need to invite a friend to question me about with regularity?

Related Readings: 2 Samuel 22:25; Job 31:4–9; Psalm 139:1–12; Revelation 2:18–23

REFLECTIONS

_____

_____

_____

_____

_____

27

FINANCIAL BOLD HUMILITY

My son, if you have put up security for your neighbor…
Go and humble yourself; press your plea with your neighbor!
Allow no sleep to your eyes, no slumber to your eyelids. Free yourself.
Proverbs 6:1, 3–5

It is hard to manage our own debt obligations, much less the debt commitment of another. Therefore, wisdom says to free yourself from financial surety so you are free to serve. It is not smart to cosign credit on behalf of another. If you do, make plans to pay what is due. Or in bold humility, go to the one for whom you partnered or cosigned, and ask if you can get out from under the financial obligation.

Even if you pay a penalty for backing out, what price would you pay for your newfound peace of mind? Financial overextension is unwise. Perhaps you should consolidate your credit and make a bold plan to pay down your personal debt. Debt reduction is smart, especially during recessionary times. The "borrower is servant to the lender" (Proverbs 22:7); so in humility and boldness you can break the chain of financial servitude.

"You were bought with a price; do not become slaves of men" (1 Corinthians 7:23 NASB).

It is countercultural to limit credit or abolish it completely. Why make credit convenient to a spender who struggles to stay within a budget? Therefore, apply discipline and sacrifice. You can experience the peaceful result of debt-free living. Perhaps in bold humility, ask your parents to match every dollar you pay toward debt reduction.

There is one other word related to cosigning. There may be a young person who needs someone to vouch for his or her character and credit. Like the apostle Paul guaranteed the servant Onesimus's repayment, you may be led to do the same for someone. Perhaps you ultimately see your assistance as a gift. So if you are paid back, it is an unexpected bonus. Relationships are much more valuable than cash. Regardless of the stressful situation, make sure you manage expectations with prayerful prudence and bold humility.

"If then you consider me a partner and a comrade in fellowship, welcome and receive him as you would [welcome and receive] me. And if he has done you any wrong in any way or owes anything [to you], charge that to my account. I, Paul, write it with my own hand, I promise to repay it [in full]" (Philemon 1:17–19 AB).

Whom do I need to boldly, but humbly, approach about dissolving a financial arrangement?

Related Readings: Proverbs 22:7; 1 Corinthians 7:23; Philemon 1:1–25

REFLECTIONS

_____

_____

_____

_____

_____

28

PLAN AHEAD

Go to the ant, you sluggard; consider its ways and be wise!
It has no commander, no overseer or ruler, yet it stores its provisions
in summer and gathers its food at harvest.
Proverbs 6:6–8

Wisdom works hard now but is wise about planning for the future.
There is an innate discipline about planners. Imminently urgent matters do not distract them as they stay focused on important issues. Their discipline determines the choices they make during the day because they are always keenly aware that their actions affect their future. The best planners take the time to process assumptions and the implications of best-case and worst-case scenarios.

Self-motivated and disciplined planners do not require rigid management and control. They thrive in autonomy but still submit to the accountability of authority. Wise planners save time and money. There is a decision-making filter in place that results in more noes than yeses to good opportunities. The Holy Spirit works through a prayerfully crafted plan to guide you into God's best; so stay aligned with the plan.

"Many are the plans in a person's heart, but it is the LORD'S purpose that prevails" (Proverbs 19:21).

Ants are small in stature, but the unified effort of many is large in results. A clearly defined, well-executed plan brings your team together and produces an outstanding outcome. A plan creates credibility and gives courage to those who implement it. So be sensitive to your season of strategic service. If you are in the preparation phase, be patient and focused on the plan.

If you are in the execution phase, remain diligent and focused on the task at hand. As you harvest success, make sure to save for the future. Abundance is not meant to be spent all at once but to be saved for the downtimes. Use your church, business, or home as a platform of provision for others in need. You plan ahead so you can be an ambassador for almighty God.

"Instruct them to do good, to be rich in good works, to be generous and ready to share, storing up for themselves the treasure of a good foundation for the future, so that they may take hold of that which is life indeed" (1 Timothy 6:18–19 NASB).

What opportunities do I need to put on hold so I can focus on implementing the current strategic plan with excellence?

Related Readings: Genesis 41:28–43; Job 12:7–8; Luke 14:28; Hebrews 6:12

☩

REFLECTIONS

_____

_____

_____

_____

_____

29

DETEST DISSENSION

There are six things the LORD hates, seven that are detestable
to him: a false witness who pours out lies and a man
who stirs up dissension among brothers.
Proverbs 6:16, 19

**The Lord loathes liars and those who stir up dissension because
they are masters at sowing seeds of doubt, deception, and discord.**
Dissenters think the worst of others and pose prideful questions like the
following: "Is he or she really fit for the job?" "Do they have honest
intentions?" "Can this person really be trusted?" Those who stir up
dissension project their own insecure feelings on the person they are seeking
to discredit or even destroy.

Like Saul, their own anger, hurt, and jealousy drive them to delusionary conclusions. It is sad to see them suffer under their own mental anguish, absent
of trust in the Lord. Their perspective becomes man-centered, while faith in
Christ is jettisoned as irrelevant. Those who stir up dissension need to be dealt
with directly, with a heart of compassion.

"The hot-tempered stir up dissension, but those who are patient calm a
quarrel" (Proverbs 15:18 TNIV).

Therefore, confront in love those who orchestrate doubt and division among
the team. Question their facts; ask them to refrain from gossip and divisive
behavior. Lastly, look into your own heart to make sure you are not guilty of lies
and deceit. Do not become like your accuser and discredit your integrity. We
see shortcomings in others because we struggle with the same familiar sins.

It is cause for humility as we seek the Lord's strength and forgiveness. By
God's grace turn mischief into maturity, discord into concord, contentiousness
into community, and pride into peace. Use your influence to lead yourself and

your team to a higher standard of conduct sanctioned by your Lord Jesus. Conflict with the contentious is meant to grow your character. Hate what the Lord hates while loving offenders through the process.

"When a man's ways are pleasing to the LORD, he makes even his enemies live at peace with him" (Proverbs 16:7).

Whom do I need to confront in love about their divisive behavior?

Related Readings: 1 Samuel 26:1–25; Proverbs 22:10; 26:20; James 3:14–16; 3 John

REFLECTIONS

_____

_____

_____

_____

_____

30

LUSTFUL LONGINGS

Do not lust in your heart after her beauty
or let her captivate you with her eyes.
Proverbs 6:25

Lustful longings lead us away from loving the Lord because our affections become attached to something that is not ours. Indeed, our emotions are meant for intimacy with our spouse and none other. Confiding in a beautiful person other than your spouse may feel good, but it is a pseudo solution, a problem waiting to happen.

If you are engaged in a relationship that causes your heart to race and feeds racy fantasies, you need to flee. It may mean your assistant transferring to another department at work or even letting her go. It is flirting with fire to forge ahead in relationships that enflame your lust; so douse the flames with the water of walking away and accountability.

"Can you build a fire in your lap and not burn your pants? Can you walk barefoot on hot coals and not get blisters? It is the same when you have sex with your neighbor's wife: Touch her and you'll pay for it. No excuses" (Proverbs 6:27–28 MSG).

Furthermore, the Internet can become a contributor to lustful longings, a tool for good which Satan uses for bad. Make sure others monitor your machine so your heart and mind do not meander to illicit images. Install computer software that forces you to be selective in your web surfing, producing a report to be reviewed by an accountability partner.

Moreover, make it your motivation and desire to pursue loving God and loving people. This will crowd out fleshly lusts from your heart. The Bible says, "Now flee from youthful lusts and pursue righteousness, faith, love and peace, with those who call on the Lord with a pure heart" (2 Timothy 2:22 NASB). A great kindness you can do for your soul is to distance yourself from sin and detest the sight of sin. Eyes focused on fidelity, faith, and authentic love lead to freedom empowered by the Holy Spirit.

"But I say, walk by the Spirit, and you will not carry out the desire of the flesh" (Galatians 5:16).

How can I protect my eyes from lustful images, focusing instead on the beauty of my spouse?

Related Readings: Genesis 39:8–10; Job 31:1–9; Matthew 5:28; 1 Peter 2:11

REFLECTIONS

_____

_____

_____

_____

_____

31

SELF-DESTRUCTION

But a man who commits adultery lacks judgment;
whoever does so destroys himself.
Proverbs 6:32

Lack of judgment can lead to self-destruction. There is an inherent life implosion for those who continue down the path of unwise decision making. The result of poor judgment is self-destruction, and the root of poor judgment is self-deception. Pride seems to pursue and capture those who are unwilling to understand and apply wisdom. They deceive themselves into thinking they have it all figured out without the counsel and accountability of others.

For example, adultery is poor judgment, but it is also a sequence of unwise decisions started long before the act of unfaithfulness. Stealing is poor judgment, but the feeling of desperation could have been addressed early on, inspired by personal humility and a teachable spirit. Self-destruction can be avoided with openness to Christ and wise counsel. Therefore, listen and learn from those who love you and who love the Lord.

"It is better to heed the rebuke of a wise person than to listen to the song of fools" (Ecclesiastes 7:5).

Indeed, poor judgment destroys spiritual vitality, tarnishes the trust of others, and can remove the hand of God's blessing. So how do we avoid poor judgment and its unseemly outcome? One remedy is to repent of self-sufficiency and surrender in total dependence to our Savior, the Lord Jesus Christ. The foundation of faith and hope in Him fuels our fear of Him, leverages our love for Him, and accelerates our obedience to Him. Self-denial precludes self-deception.

A second cure is to invite a reality check from those who know you well and desire good consequences for your life. Ask for their advice, and as you discover themes of timely truth, do what they suggest. Lastly, pray over God's Word, learn from its wisdom, and be transformed by its application. An abundant life awaits you as you die daily to self and come alive in Christ, as you act on wise advice, and as you marinate your mind in Scripture.

"And let not your behavior be like that of this world, but be changed and made new in mind, so that by experience you may have knowledge of the good and pleasing and complete purpose of God" (Romans 12:2 BBE).

What current decisions do I face that require the wisdom of God and godly counsel from trusted advisors?

Related Readings: Genesis 41:39; 2 Samuel 12:1–14; Romans 1:22-24; 1 Corinthians 15:31–34

REFLECTIONS

_____

_____

_____

_____

_____

32

LEADERS LEARN

Say to wisdom, "You are my sister," and call understanding your kinsman.
Proverbs 7:4

Leaders are learners, but when they stop learning they cease to lead wisely. Education is an enlightened envoy for leaders who think ahead and who are engaged in effective execution. If a leader does not assess the facts of a situation and operate in reality, he loses any advantage he might possess. Circumspect living is the life of a leader who is ever learning.

A leader continually asks questions like the following: "How can we better understand what the customer wants and needs?" "How can I get out of the way as the leader, supporting the team to be successful?" "How can our organization go from good to great by integrating and sustaining industry-best practices?" Leaders who learn ask the right questions, get the most accurate answers, and are able to make the wisest decisions.

"But Jehoshaphat also said to the king of Israel, 'First seek the counsel of the LORD'" (1 Kings 22:5).

Furthermore, leaders learn by listening to the Lord and to the wisdom found in His Word. Indeed, it is not a one-time educational event but the ongoing purging of pride, pretense, and prayerlessness. Wisdom becomes a beloved sister to whom you go for counsel. Humility grows into a trusted friend with whom you can confide. The Holy Bible is your defense and armor against the assault of unwise thinking.

Therefore read, study, and apply the Word of God regularly to your life. Read books that bring out bright examples of other leaders worth emulating. Learn by listening to teachers who communicate truth with clarity and conviction. Learn from your mistakes, and do not repeat them. Learn forgiveness from your family, service from your friends, and love from your enemies.

"If you have any encouragement from being united with Christ, if any comfort from his love, if any fellowship with the Spirit, if any tenderness and compassion, then make my joy complete by being like-minded, having the same love, being one in spirit and purpose" (Philippians 2:1–2).

What life lessons do I need to currently learn so the Lord can entrust me with further educational opportunities?

Related Readings: Deuteronomy 6:6–9; Psalm 90:12; 2 Corinthians 3:3; 2 Timothy 4:13

REFLECTIONS

33

FALSE SPIRITUALITY

She took hold of him and kissed him and with a brazen face she said:
"I have fellowship offerings at home; today I fulfilled my vows."
Proverbs 7:13–14

Unfortunately, there are those who use religion to get their way.
They may be single adults who prey on unsuspecting single adults in church.
They attend church to take advantage of trusting souls. Some businessmen
use the art of Christian conversation to give the appearance of values and principles based on the Bible. However, once they make the sale or close the deal,
their self-serving and dishonest ways reveal who they really are.

One of the worst types of deception is spiritual deception—using God to get our
way. In marriage it may be the husband who uses submission to control his
wife, or it may be the wife who uses grace to withhold from her husband.
Therefore, warn those who, like Simon in the early church, try to buy the Holy
Spirit for their benefit. Cultivate authentic spirituality in your heart and mind
through prayer, worship, and community.

"Such regulations indeed have an appearance of wisdom, with their self-
imposed worship, their false humility and their harsh treatment of the body,
but they lack any value in restraining sensual indulgence" (Colossians 2:23).

True spirituality, on the other hand, is motivated and controlled by the Spirit of
Christ. There is authenticity because almighty God is the initiator. True
spirituality is not just looking out for itself but is sincerely concerned with
serving others. You are comfortable with them because you know they care for
you. Integrity rises from their business and religious activities.

Their yes is their yes, and their no is their no. There are no surprises; what you
see is what you get. True spirituality comes over time. It is forged on the anvil

of adversity, taught at the hearth of humility, and received at the gate of God's grace. You know your religion is real when you love others above your needs and you care for the poor and needy. True spirituality leads others to love God and obey His commands.

"Pure and undefiled religion in the sight of our God and Father is this: to visit orphans and widows in their distress, and to keep oneself unstained by the world" (James 1:27 NASB).

Whom do I need to confront in love about using their "Christianity" to take advantage of others?

Related Readings: Ecclesiastes 7:4; Matthew 25:36; Acts 8:19–20; 2 Corinthians 1:17

REFLECTIONS

_____

_____

_____

_____

_____

34

TRAVEL TEMPTATIONS

My husband is not at home; he has gone on a long journey.
He took his purse filled with money and will not be home till full moon."
Proverbs 7:19–20

Wise men and women meditate on God. Conversely, what is your behavior when you are the spouse left back at home? Is your house a palace of peace or a prison of confinement? Not only must the weary traveler be wary of wrong behavior, but so must the one left holding down the fort. Perhaps as a couple you craft together guidelines defining what you will and will not do while separated by travel.

Distance can grow the heart fonder and more faithful or fire the flames of lust and infidelity. If you travel for your work, you most likely are motivated to meet the needs of your family. However, every assignment is for a season. Maybe it is time to get off the road and reconnect with your child who is approaching the teen years, or be there more often for your spouse who is starved for extra emotional support. Just be willing to adjust.

"Do not be misled: 'Bad company corrupts good character.' Come back to your senses as you ought, and stop sinning; for there are some who are ignorant of God—I say this to your shame" (1 Corinthians 15:33–34).

Moreover, do not drift into travel temptations that become divisive and deteriorate your marriage. One boundary may be to avoid bars and get back to your room soon after work and dinner. A righteous routine on the road gets the right results. Whenever it is possible, make it a priority to travel with another person of similar values. Be bold by becoming an influencer of integrity: good, clean fun without flirting with sin. On the other hand, your role in the marriage may be to support the children and manage the home daily. Take pride, not pity, during this season of unselfish service.

By God's grace you are molding their minds to the things of Christ, influencing the culture with His kingdom priorities. As you are working to preserve the family, you are as valuable as the one out working to provide for the family. Stay occupied in prayer, Bible study, and their school, and be available to those who need you. Marriage is a team effort that sees outstanding results when you are both on the same page of love and obedience to Christ. Travel temptations are terminated on both ends through trust in the Lord and trust in each other.

"He trusts in the LORD; let the LORD rescue him. Let him deliver him, since he delights in him" (Psalm 22:8).

What behavioral boundaries related to our time apart do I need to cocreate with my spouse?

Related Readings: Numbers 5:11–15; Isaiah 46:6; Luke 12:39–46; 1 John 3:9

✺

REFLECTIONS

35

RAISING SONS

Listen, my son, to your father's instruction
and do not forsake your mother's teaching.
Proverbs 1:8

Raising a son requires intentionality from a parent or parents. Wise are the father and mother who have a plan to instruct and teach their son how to make God-honoring choices and to lead like Jesus. Yes, being an excellent example is fundamental, but it takes more than modeling—sons need to understand the whys, whats and hows.

For example, they need life preparation in how to become a Christian, pray, and study the Bible and to take them through the book of John to love Jesus, the book of Ephesians to grasp grace, and the book of Proverbs to embrace wisdom. Boys and young men who grow up fearing God are prepared to persevere through adversity, success, marriage, and parenting.

"Listen to your father, who gave you life, and do not despise your mother when she is old. Buy the truth and do not sell it—wisdom, instruction and insight as well" (Proverbs 23:22-23).

Fathers, show your son how to relate to girls and young women by loving and cherishing your wife—and, wives, be an example of the woman he will marry by respecting and following your husband. Parents who agree in their discipline and expectations provide a consistent environment that causes their son to grow in confidence and manhood.

Anger does not work in molding your son's will; rather use encouragement and calm correction. Lead him to be accountable to almighty God, and then he will behave well, even when you are absent from his presence. Teach him the value of hard work. Let your son sweat through manual labor. Help him discover his God-given gifts, and then invest time and money to develop his skills. Competence and character create confidence.

"Listen, my son, and be wise, and set your heart on the right path" (Proverbs 23:19).

What if your son strays from the truth? What if he makes a series of foolish decisions? It is imperative dad and mom stay on their knees in earnest prayer for their wayward son. Pray for him to be influenced by those who love Christ, pray for him to grow weary of sin, and pray for the love of God to draw him to Himself. Parents' prayers are productive.

Rules without relationship lead to rebellion; so keep your relationship growing, and communicate often. Even if you are the only one initiating, stay the course in caring correspondence. Above all, start early instilling godly wisdom into your son, as it is easier to build sons than to fix sons. Lead him to be a leader who loves God. Indeed, joy awaits the parent or parents who by God's grace are able to grow up godly sons.

"The father of a righteous child has great joy; a man who fathers a wise son rejoices in him. May your father and mother rejoice; may she who gave you birth be joyful!" (Proverbs 23:24-25).

Am I intentional in how I raise my son in the ways of the Lord?

Related Readings: Proverbs 23:15-16; 31:2; Philippians 2:22; James 2:21

REFLECTIONS

36

WISDOM SPEAKS OUT

Does not wisdom call out? Does not understanding raise her voice?
On the heights along the way, where the paths meet, she takes her stand.
Proverbs 8:1–2

Wisdom is not shy; it proclaims itself and speaks out in public places. Like the Lord speaking to Moses on Mount Sinai, He spoke wisdom loudly with authority, clarity, and finality, and like John the Baptist, who boldly cried out repentance and faith in Christ to the crowds. Wisdom is not a secret secluded in solitary confinement waiting to be let out. It calls out publicly and openly.

Because wisdom is so easily accessible, it is imperative we listen and learn from its instruction. Sunday morning teaching at your church should be a reservoir of wisdom. If not, consider transferring to a fellowship where access to truth is easy to find. Wisdom drowns out the whispers of gossiping fools because wisdom has the last word. Listen for wisdom, and you will learn how to follow the Lord.

"He proclaimed the kingdom of God and taught about the Lord Jesus Christ—with all boldness and without hindrance!" (Acts 28:31).

The way of wisdom works because it invites God's blessing. For example, financial wisdom is to avoid debt, save, and pay cash. Relational wisdom is listening with understanding to another's needs, repeating back what you heard, confirming your comprehension, and, if appropriate, offering ideas that may bring benefit. Parenting wisdom is finding couples whose children are upright and learning from them. Business wisdom is building your enterprise on honesty and integrity, not compromising your convictions for cash.

Wisdom has worthy things to say; so listen for it each day and learn. Train your ears to listen for wisdom in sermons and everyday conversations. Expose your eyes to wisdom in books and the Bible. Lastly, look for wise behavior to emulate from those who enjoy the fruit of faithful living. Wisdom speaks out so you can live it out.

"Wisdom shouts in the street, She lifts her voice in the square"
(Proverbs 1:20 NASB).

Where is wisdom trying to get my attention, and how can I apply its truth?

Related Readings: Exodus 19:1–25; Isaiah 58:1; Matthew 3:3; John 7:37; Hebrews 12:25

REFLECTIONS

37

HATE EVIL

To fear the Lord is to hate evil; I hate pride and arrogance,
evil behavior and perverse speech."
Proverbs 8:13

The word hate makes us uncomfortable. It has a harsh and uncaring ring and reputation. However, there is a holy hatred of evil that is allowed and even expected by almighty God. Authentic Christianity is not easy on evil, which breaks the heart of God and destroys the soul of man. Evil is an encroachment by the enemy on eternity's agenda. It takes down leaders who let pride and arrogance seep into their thick skulls and stay there.

Indeed, if the rules apply to everyone but the leader, then it is just a matter of time before the fear of the Lord becomes a foreign concept. Sin is out-of-bounds for any child of God who abounds in the love and grace of God. It is the wisdom of Christ that warms the heart, instructs the mind, and leads the way into behavior defined by truth.

"God's mystery, that is, Christ Himself, in whom are hidden all the treasures of wisdom and knowledge" (Colossians 2:2–3 NASB).

Gossip, greed, jealousy, and lies are all evil intentions that corrupt a culture of transparency, generosity, contentment, and honesty. Stress can bring out the best and worst in others; so make sure, by the grace of God, you rise above the petty politics of blame. Wisdom and maturity seek responsibility to lead the team in excellent execution of a proven strategy. If you do nothing, then the naysayers will negotiate for fear and division.

Furthermore, fight evil without fanfare, but by faith and wise work, deliver constant, creditable results, and your antagonists will grow quiet. It is the humility and wisdom of Christ that defeat evil initiatives. Therefore, give Him the glory, get the job done, and trust the Lord with the results. Hard times can produce hard hearts unless you overcome evil with a humble heart of prayer and bold faith. Evil is extinguished under intense intercession of prayers from pure people.

"Make this your common practice: Confess your sins to each other and pray for each other so that you can live together whole and healed. The prayer of a person living right with God is something powerful to be reckoned with" (James 5:16–17 MSG).

What does a holy hatred of evil look like in my life?

Related Readings: Amos 5:15; Zechariah 8:17; Romans 12:9; 2 Timothy 2:19

♛

REFLECTIONS

_____

_____

_____

_____

_____

38

POLITICAL WISDOM

"By me [wisdom] kings reign and rulers make laws that are just;
by me princes govern, and all nobles who rule on earth."
Proverbs 8:15–16

The wisdom of God overshadows the best and brightest thinking of man. This is why our ancestors accessed the Almighty for knowledge and understanding in crafting our constitution. Its remarkable effectiveness is contingent on faith: faith in God, faith in government, and faith in its citizens. Indeed, politicians who plead with Providence for wisdom will become the wiser. Rulers who recognize their authority is from God will rule for God.

There is a humble ambition that escorts the most effective statesman into public service, as political pride is exchanged for humble wisdom. Those rule wisely in whom religion rules in their conscience and character. Political wisdom is a prerequisite for those public servants who govern in alignment with the principles of Providence on behalf of the people. These wise rulers are able to rest in peace in the middle of a storm.

"For the one in authority is God's servant for your good. But if you do wrong, be afraid, for rulers do not bear the sword for no reason. They are God's servants, agents of wrath to bring punishment on the wrongdoer" (Romans 13:4).

A culture thrown into economic chaos especially needs principled men and women to step up, sacrifice, and make hard decisions. Wisdom in the middle of extreme uncertainty requires painful prescriptions to prevent further panic. Wise politicians face disastrous consequences and determine what is best for the whole in light of the long term. Pray for political leaders to look beyond themselves and only short-term relief into the perspective and principles of God found in Holy Scripture.

Indeed, political wisdom prays for intervention and understanding from the Almighty. Perhaps during desperate days a filibuster of faith is first needed; so our leaders start by looking and listening to the Lord. Just laws follow political wisdom, which does what is right as Christ defines right. Wise politicians keep their hands of faithfulness on the Bible's principles and their hearts submitted under the Lord's authority. Presidents honor Him by never forgetting their inaugural sacred vow, "So help me God."

"Blessed be the LORD your God who delighted in you to set you on the throne of Israel; because the LORD loved Israel forever, therefore He made you king, to do justice and righteousness" (1 Kings 10:9 NASB).

How can I facilitate political wisdom with those public servants in my circle of influence?

Related Readings: Psalm 148:11–13; Daniel 2:21–47; Romans 13:1; Revelation 19:11–16

REFLECTIONS

_____

_____

_____

_____

_____

39

WISDOM IS CREATIVE

"The LORD brought me [wisdom] forth as the first of his works,
before his deeds of old…. Then I was the craftsman at his side.
I was filled with delight day after day, rejoicing always in his presence."
Proverbs 8:22, 30

Wisdom predates the creation. Like Jesus, it was with God from the beginning. Wisdom is the Lord's instrument of creativity and beauty. It stands by His side as a craftsman ever ready to create for the cause of Christ. Indeed, it is from heavenly inspired wisdom that we experience creative earthly results. Wisdom longs for you to look for better ways to complement your calling by prayerfully engaging the Lord's limitless resources.

The creative energy of wisdom does not sit still but seeks out other meaningful methods and models. If how you did something in the past is not effective in the present, put it to rest and watch the Holy Spirit reengineer. What will it take for you to let go of control and be creative? The best people leave entrenched environments lacking creativity; however, wise is the leader who invites innovation.

"He [the Lord] has filled him with the Spirit of God, with wisdom, with understanding, with knowledge and with all kinds of skills—to make artistic designs for work in gold, silver and bronze" (Exodus 35:31–32).

Furthermore, there is a joy and an anticipation that accompany creativity. You feel fulfilled and significant when you create a product or process that achieves excellent results. Wisdom at work creates a system that rewards creative thinking around relationships and results. Remain creative and live; lose creativity and die. Indeed, intense adversity invites lavish creativity; so be wise, and use hard times to harness ingenuity. Challenge team members to create compelling content rich in substance, affordable in price, and easily accessible.

Above all else, tap into the wisdom and creativity of Christ. Eternity explodes in colorful creativity that birthed the universe. Go to Jesus and seek His mind for new and imaginative thinking. Prayer gives you permission to invent and innovate. Unleash wisdom and experience the Technicolor creativity of Christ. Partner with your Creator, and by faith and wisdom create for the cause of Christ.

"O LORD, how many are Your works! In wisdom You have made them all; The earth is full of Your possessions" (Psalm 104:24 NASB).

By faith, what do I need to stop doing, being more creative with a new and more affordable model?

Related Readings: Exodus 39:43; Proverbs 3:19; Hebrews 1:12; Colossians 1:16

REFLECTIONS

40

GOD'S FAVOR

"Blessed is the man who listens to me [wisdom], watching daily
at my doors, waiting at my doorway. For whoever finds me
finds life and receives favor from the Lord."
Proverbs 8:34–35

God's favor is the fruit of friends who find wisdom. They seek wisdom by first watching at the doors of heaven, waiting patiently at the feet of their Savior Jesus. It is humbling to think that each day almighty God is available to commission our cause for Christ. The wisdom of Jesus is what we pursue because His is pure and profound.

Like Able, the Almighty looks for the best offering for blessing. Therefore, honor God by offering Him the firstfruits of your day. Just as He deserves first dibs on your money, so He expects the beginning of your day. Get up and go to God first. There you discover a wealth of wisdom, and under the shadow of your Savior Jesus Christ you receive His favor.

"Then that person can pray to God and find favor with him, they will see God's face and shout for joy; he will restore them to full well-being" (Job 33:26).

Happiness happens to those who wait for wisdom. His blessing cannot be rushed; so rest in Him. The favor of God is well worth the wait; like a newborn, the joy is unspeakable. How many times have we rushed ahead, outside the canopy of Christ's blessing? The Israelites learned to stay under the cloud of God and be led by faith. Indeed, there is no spiritual oxygen to sustain those in an out-of-favor environment. It is lifeless and lonely. However, for those on whom their heavenly Father's favor rests, there is rest.

His blessing provides strength for the journey and perseverance to stay on the trail of trust. Jesus experienced the favor of His heavenly Father when He submitted to public baptism—His confession of faith, His commitment to public service, His commission to ministry. On what issue of obedience do you need wisdom to continually experience the favor of your heavenly Father? Your life is alive and vibrant because the Lord favors you. You are a favorite of your heavenly Father because you are learning to wait on Him and to humbly walk with the wise.

"He has told you, O man, what is good; And what does the LORD require of you But to do justice, to love kindness, And to walk humbly with your God?" (Micah 6:8 NASB).

How can I make sure I stay in a position to receive God's favor and blessing?

Related Readings: Genesis 4:4; Exodus 33:12; Luke 2:52; Philippians 3:8

REFLECTIONS

_____

_____

_____

_____

_____

41

RICH PROVISION

Wisdom has built her house; she has hewn out its seven pillars.
She has prepared her meat and mixed her wine; she has also set her table.
Proverbs 9:1–2

Wisdom is the pathway to God's rich provision. His Holy Spirit allows you to see the common with uncommon eyes, thus coming up with creative alternatives. Wisdom is the Lord's way of preparing plenty of resources and relationships for you to further His will. He readily sends forth His Holy Spirit for discernment of people and insight into situations.

Therefore, ask the Lord for understanding in what to do and what not to do. When God gives you the green light, go forward in faith, knowing He will provide. He has prepared a place for you, not only in heaven but also on earth. Wisdom's preparations are plentiful and pretty. So be patient, do the next wise thing, and watch God work in ways you never imagined. Wisdom is at work on behalf of your work.

"The one who gets wisdom loves life; the one who cherishes understanding will soon prosper" (Proverbs 19:8).

Maybe He is calling you to worship and community with different followers of Christ. A church built on the foundation of God's wisdom is the best preparation for your faith and family. Yes, you are best fed in a family of faith where the Word of God is given full attention and examination. Like the Bereans in the early church, you are encouraged to boldly ask questions relating to the meaning of Scripture.

The church is God's house for prayer and the proclamation of His principles for the gaining of wisdom to live life. Thus, gather wisdom every chance you get, and you will become rich indeed: rich in relationships, rich in character, rich in robust relationship with Jesus, and maybe rich in stuff. Wisdom is at work on your behalf; so tap into its rich provision.

"For every house is built by someone, but the builder of all things is God" (Hebrews 3:4 NASB).

Where is the wisdom of God preparing His provision that I need to access by faith?

Related Readings: Genesis 43:16; Acts 17:10–12; 1 Timothy 3:15; 1 Corinthians 3:9–15

REFLECTIONS

_____

_____

_____

_____

_____

42

CHOOSE YOUR BATTLES

"Whoever corrects a mocker invites insult;
whoever rebukes a wicked man incurs abuse."
Proverbs 9:7

We all have a limited amount of time and energy. Wisdom says to spend them both on productive people, not destructive ones. Verbal sparring with those who are proud only invites insult. It is better to ignore their venomous venting than try to reason with them. Do your best, stay focused on the task, and trust your reputation with the giver of reputations—your Savior Jesus.

Mockers look to stir up things in the moment. They have no long-term solutions; so avoid their cynical, crazy cycle. A mocker's mind is already made up; he will not change regardless of wise rationale. There are those who return evil for good; so do not go there, or you may end up in despair. Jesus says the caustic cynic is full of pride.

"Let them alone; they are blind guides of the blind. And if a blind man guides a blind man, both will fall into a pit" (Matthew 15:14 NASB).

Furthermore, what about a family member who seems to be hurtling down a path of destruction? Specifically, you may have a teenager or adult child whose entire focus is friends and freedom. They seem to have rejected all common sense and Christlike influences. First and foremost, focus on their heart with love and acceptance. If you battle over the external, it will be messy and costly. However, if they change from the inside out, the transformation will be beautiful and enduring.

Ask them to pray, asking the Lord what He thinks about their decisions and choice of friends. Direct them back to Scripture as their Savior's standard for living. Above all, pursue a peaceful and patient attitude in prayer. Our most significant battles are spiritual; they are won or lost on our knees. The Holy Spirit will lead you when to speak, what to say, and when to remain silent. Everyone wins when you value the relationship over winning the argument.

"Do not rebuke a mocker or he will hate you; rebuke a wise man and he will love you" (Proverbs 9:8).

What relationship do I need to quit striving over and give to the Lord?

Related Readings: 2 Chronicles 30:7–9; Proverbs 23:9; Matthew 7:6; 22:4–6

REFLECTIONS

43

INVITE INSTRUCTION

"Rebuke a wise man and he will love you. Instruct a wise man and he
will be wiser still; teach a righteous man and he will add to his learning."
Proverbs 9:8–9

Wise people invite instruction. They understand correction and rebuke
are necessary to grow in wisdom and righteous behavior. Without well-mean-
ing instructors willing to get in our faces, we aspire to average at best.
However, an invitation to mettle in my affairs defines authentic accountability.
Effective correction makes us uncomfortable at times, but we become wiser
as a result. Indeed, conflict is inherent in accountability.

So if your relationships are conflict free, you can bet you are not being held
accountable in the truest sense. Wisdom comes in the form of raw
relationships that reek with loving reproof and willingness to change. It is out
of a rebuke that you wake up and understand the realities you are facing. Your
spouse is not nagging, just nudging you to act responsibly. Therefore, invite
instruction, and you will increase in wisdom and understanding. There are no
regrets from wise recipients of reproof.

"Like an earring of gold or an ornament of fine gold is the rebuke of a wise
judge to a listening ear" (Proverbs 25:12).

Furthermore, be willing to be the bearer of bad news. With love and grace, go
to your friend who has asked for your counsel, and give him or her truth. Pray
first; then deliver the unpleasant news. It is much better for others to see the
error of their ways before they reach a point of no return. Talk to them, not
about them. Pray for them privately, not publically with a pious prayer request.

Love motivates rebuke and then becomes a recipient of love. Your relationship
will retreat in anger or rise to a higher level of respect through righteous

rebuke. Take the time to prod another toward perfection because you care. Be respectful; instruct with patience. One day the student may exceed the wisdom of the teacher.

"A student is not above his teacher, but everyone who is fully trained will be like his teacher" (Luke 6:40).

To whom do I need to listen, learning from their correction and rebuke?

Related Readings: Psalm 141:5; 2 Peter 3:18; 2 Timothy 4:2; Revelation 3:19

REFLECTIONS

_____

_____

_____

_____

_____

44

BEGINNING OF WISDOM

The fear of the Lord is the beginning of wisdom,
and knowledge of the Holy One is understanding."
Proverbs 9:10

The fear of the Lord is fundamental to finding wisdom. Without awe of the Almighty, there is no access to His insights. Where reverence for His holiness is void, there is lack of understanding into the ways of God. The first step in acquiring wisdom from almighty God is to fear Him. There is a worship of the Lord's majesty and a dread of His judgment.

His Holy Word—the Bible—is taken to heart as truth for the purpose of life transformation. At first, fear of the Lord may be so overwhelming that it casts out love and distracts our desire for intimacy. Anyone who has been broken understands this process. However, once a healthy fear of the Lord has been embraced, the result is peace and knowledge in submission to and love for the Holy One.

"He will be the sure foundation for your times, a rich store of salvation and wisdom and knowledge; the fear of the LORD is the key to this treasure" (Isaiah 33:6).

Moreover, we mock God when we move away from the language of fear; He is not one to be mocked. So as devoted followers of Christ, we sow the seeds of respect, reverence, and fear of the Lord. This discipline of faith results in a harvest of holiness, happiness, and wisdom. Fear of Him leads to knowledge of Him. Therefore, bowing before Him on your knees in prayer, seek His face for forgiveness and relational restoration.

Celebrate together with Christ our conquest over sin, sorrow, and death. What is counterintuitive on earth is intuitive in heaven. Listen to David admonish his son Solomon, who became the wisest man in the world: "As for you, my son Solomon, know the God of your father, and serve Him with a whole heart and a willing mind; for the LORD searches all hearts, and understands every intent of the thoughts. If you seek Him, He will let you find Him; but if you forsake Him, He will reject you forever" (1 Chronicles 28:9 NASB).

What area of my life lacks fear of the Lord, and how can I expose it to accountability?

Related Readings: Job 28:28; Psalm 111:10; Matthew 11:27; 1 John 5:20

REFLECTIONS

_____

_____

_____

_____

_____

45

FLIRTATIOUS FOLLY

The woman Folly is loud; she is undisciplined
and without knowledge.
Proverbs 9:13

What is flirtatious folly? It is enticement into reckless living. You may ask, "What does it look like?" Its coyness is conceived in attractive idiots, as these disguised fools seek to lure naïve ones into their stupidity. Foolishness loves friends. It approaches in the form of a well-dressed, well-spoken man or woman who draws you in with his or her looks and latches on to you with his or her words.

Folly can be found among the experienced and educated or run rampant in lives of the young and simple. It forces itself on the middle-aged father who has grown discontent with his faith, family, and vocation. Instead of listening to the voice of reason, he socializes with silliness and invites irresponsibility. However, he does not harvest happiness because the fruit of folly is death: relational, spiritual, and emotional.

"She caught him by his cloak and said, 'Come to bed with me!' But he left his cloak in her hand and ran out of the house" (Genesis 39:12).

Moreover, wise men and women recognize the futility of folly and flee from its influence. They avoid sexual folly by cultivating a caring marriage. A happy wife is a happy life, and a happy husband is a happy home. Furthermore, financial folly is fleeting for a family who lives well within their means, growing in generosity. Their money becomes a means of honoring their Master Jesus (see Matthew 6:21).

What form of folly is staring you in the face? Wisdom is your warning to flee where good judgment is absent. It may require changing schools, breaking off a relationship, or moving to another neighborhood. Wisdom may not be sexy, but it brings success and satisfaction. Walk in wisdom, and you will reap rich relationships, robust faith, and peace of mind.

"I will listen to what God the LORD will say; he promises peace to his people, his saints—but let them not return to folly" (Psalm 85:8).

Where do I need to force folly from my life, replacing it with wisdom and discernment?

Related Readings: Job 2:9–10; Proverbs 21:9–19; James 1:13–15; 2 Peter 2:18–21

REFLECTIONS

46

ILL-GOTTEN TREASURES

Ill-gotten treasures are of no value,
but righteousness delivers from death.
Proverbs 10:2

Ill-gotten treasures insult integrity in the process of procuring profit. It is money manipulated by man rather than blessed by God. There is no profit for the soul because the means by which the money was made was centered on self, not on the Savior Jesus. He clearly addresses this: "For what does it profit a man if he gains the whole world and forfeits his soul? Or what will a man give in exchange for his soul?" (Matthew 16:26 NASB).

Indeed, the method and motive for making money do matter. Can financial integrity be assured without transparency in our business dealings or personal financial management? Does God wink at our wrong ways when we attach aggressive giving to ill-gotten gain? We need to be careful not to allow the end of philanthropy to justify the means of dishonesty. However, honestly earned treasures display the hand of heaven on your head. You can go to the bank and thank God along the way.

So how do we know if our acquired treasures are legitimate, as the Lord defines legitimate? One indicator is the extent of His blessing, for God blesses benevolence birthed out of brokenness and honest work. For example, you invite trustworthiness when there is full disclosure in financial reporting. It may mean losing a deal, but the Lord can lead you to better, even more lucrative, opportunities.

Moreover, treat others as you want to be treated. Jesus said, "Do to others as you would have them do to you" (Luke 6:31). Thus, you avoid intimidation, fear tactics, and disrespectful attitudes. God blesses respect.

Lastly, a company with a Christlike culture is attractive. You do not have to look over your shoulder because you know other team members cover your back. Indeed, honesty is the best policy in producing profit. Untainted treasure comes from trusting God. It matters as much how you make it as how you give it away.

"Make sure that your character is free from the love of money" (Hebrews 13:5 NASB).

Where is my character being tempted to compromise for the sake of cash, and how can I make sure I behave correctly?

Related Readings: Job 36:19; Psalm 49:6–10; Luke 12:15–21; James 5:1–3

REFLECTIONS

_____

_____

_____

_____

_____

47

LOVE FORGIVES

Hatred stirs up dissension, but love covers over all wrongs.
Proverbs 10:12

True love forgives, regardless of the infraction, because it transcends mistreatment. So what is your process for forgiveness? Is it conditional, based on the way you are treated, or is it unconditional? Hatred has no hope but to stir up dissension and rally a defense. However, love looks at being wronged as an opportunity to replace insult with encouragement. Love seeks to lead all parties into a better place of health and happiness.

Indeed, hatred is not at home in a heart of love. It sows discord, while love plants peace. It embraces enmity, while love cuddles compassion. Hate stirs up, but love calms down. How do you handle those who are hard to be around? Perhaps out of love you serve them. Seek to serve rather than be served.

"Through love serve one another" (Galatians 5:13 NASB).

Furthermore, love forgives because you have been forgiven by the matchless love of God. It is the Lord's love toward you that empowers you to lovingly forgive another. Human love alone is unable to love without boundaries. Left to our own limited love, we only love those who love us. Jesus said, "If you love only those who love you, what reward is there for that? Even corrupt tax collectors do that much" (Matthew 5:46 NLT).

Therefore, look at love as an opportunity to give others what they do not deserve. Lean on the Lord as your source of unconditional love. Christ's love is all-inclusive and all-forgiving. In the same way, actively and appropriately love those in your life, maybe with a kind word, a nice note of appreciation, a thoughtful gift, or a listening ear. How do you harness love into a habit of forgiveness?

"Most important of all, continue to show deep love for each other, for love covers a multitude of sins" (1 Peter 4:8 NLT).

Whom do I need to love, forgive, and serve in honor of God's great love?

Related Readings: Leviticus 19:17; Proverbs 17:9; Philippians 1:9; 1 John 4:20–21

REFLECTIONS

_____

_____

_____

_____

_____

48

TEMPERED TALK

When words are many, sin is not absent,
but he who holds his tongue is wise.
Proverbs 10:19

Tempered talk is evidence of wise conversation. It is when our words are many that we run the risk of soliciting sin. Increased words increase the probability of improper speech. For example, respectful conversation does not repeat the same words and phrases in a confined period of time. This impatient cadence frustrates.

Perhaps a look of misunderstanding requires questions for clarification or definitions for comprehension. Proud conversationalists can highjack a listener's understanding with a hoard of words without meaning. If your goal is to communicate, then take the time to listen to the needs of your audience. People who feel cared for and understood have a keener sense of hearing and understanding.

"Even a fool is thought wise if he keeps silent, and discerning if he holds his tongue" (Proverbs 17:28).

Wise people weigh their words before they speak. They allow their minds to catch up with their hearts. Furthermore, in the face of wrong behavior, emotions sometimes need to express themselves. Let the other person know if you feel mistreated or misinformed. Concealed anger leads to living a lie (see Proverbs 10:18), but tempered talk is truthful and to the point.

Lastly, you reserve your words out of respect for the other person. If you do all the talking, you are the center of attention. It is condescending conversation when the other individual does not feel important enough to speak up. So honor others by speaking less, listening more intently to how you can love them. Wisdom can be found in the words of each person you meet. Therefore, intentionally talk less and be wise.

"My dear brothers, take note of this: Everyone should be quick to listen, slow to speak and slow to become angry" (James 1:19).

Whom do I need to listen to more and talk less?

Related Readings: Job 2:3; Amos 5:13; Titus 1:10; James 3:2

REFLECTIONS

_____

_____

_____

_____

_____

49

ECONOMIC STORM

When the storm has swept by, the wicked are gone,
but the righteous stand firm forever.
Proverbs 10:25

Economic storms expose evil, as when the ocean tide goes out, you are able to see those naked in the water. Dead wood is swept away, no more to be seen. It may seem like the wicked are prospering, but eventually they will be found out. The Holy Spirit shakes out sin so it can be seen and judged. As the Lord promised His children in the past, "I will shake the house of Israel" (Amos 9:9).

What use is it to make a lot of noise, draw the attention of the elite, and then lose your creditability under scrutiny? Economic storms collapse businesses and ministries that are dependent on debt and, conversely, cause good churches to increase in attendance. There is a purging of pride, and all manner of excess is exposed. What really matters in life becomes the priority: faith, family, friends, food, and shelter. Storms reveal worth.

Moreover, those who cling to Christ are not shaken. He is our cornerstone, which no degree of chaos can challenge. The righteous cannot be moved because their Master is immovable. Therefore, stand firm in the Lord.

"Those who trust in the LORD are like Mount Zion, which cannot be shaken but endures forever" (Psalm 125:1).

Worldly wisdom has a way of reducing heaven's wisdom to an afterthought. After using our worldly wisdom, we pray, seeking to discern the Lord's ways, but only after our ways do not work. It is tempting to rely on what seems to work instead of asking what principles to live by based on God's economy.

Furthermore, your stability in your Savior is security for your family, friends, and work associates. Your unwavering faith during difficult days helps them replace panic with peace, fear with faith, and compromise with conviction. Indeed, if all you have left is a firm foundation of faith, begin rebuilding God's big vision. Are you a wise builder?

"Therefore everyone who hears these words of mine and puts them into practice is like a wise man who built his house on the rock" (Matthew 7:24).

How can I build my life, home, and work on the solid rock of Jesus?

Related Readings: Job 20:5; Psalm 37:10; Acts 2:25; Hebrews 12:28

REFLECTIONS

50

RIGHTEOUS RESOLVE

The righteous will never be uprooted,
but the wicked will not remain in the land.
Proverbs 10:30

Resolve is the result of righteous living. There is a determination deep within a soul dependent on God. When you are established in the faith, no one can move you away from Christ's call. He has appointed you to this post of service. Do not leave until the Lord reassigns you. Righteous resolve decides to stay put; so by faith keep on for Christ.

You will likely disappoint some and invigorate others. However, if your goal is to first trust and obey the Lord, you will be misunderstood by some and rejected by others. Friends may even urge you to move on, but you cannot because Christ has not released you. Your resolve is His resolve. Therefore, you persevere through pain, suffering, and uncertainty. Righteous resolve remains, regardless of the consequences, good or bad.

"But Daniel resolved not to defile himself with the royal food and wine, and he asked the chief official for permission not to defile himself this way" (Daniel 1:8).

Moreover, there is a righteous resolve that remains in Christ (see John 15:5). Your conversion to Christianity was a resolution to abide under the influence of almighty God. You stay true to your commitment to Christ because of the joy that comes from following Jesus. "The meek...inherit the earth" (Matthew 5:5), while the wicked do not.

Lastly, you cannot lose what you give away, and you cannot keep what you will not release. Indeed, a righteous resolve has a relentless trust in the Lord. Obedience, generosity, and contentment all require tenacious trust. Therefore, resolve in your heart to go hard after God. Release your relentless pursuits only after He has released you. Perhaps you ask, "Is my resolve righteous, or is it contingent on circumstances?"

"Alarmed, Jehoshaphat resolved to inquire of the LORD" (2 Chronicles 20:3).

Where do I need a righteous resolve to remain true to my commitment and calling?

Related Readings: Psalm 15:5; Romans 8:35–39; 1 Corinthians 2:2

REFLECTIONS

_____

_____

_____

_____

_____

51

FAITHFUL GUIDE

The integrity of the upright guides them,
but the unfaithful are destroyed by their duplicity.
Proverbs 11:3

Integrity is an instrument of almighty God. He uses it to guide His children in the direction He desires for them. Have you ever wondered what God would have you do? Integrity is His directive to do the next right thing, trusting Him with the results. It is out of our honesty we begin to comprehend Christ's desires. He delights in our uprightness.

For example, are you totally honest on your tax return? Is your tax preparer a person of unquestionable integrity? We can trust professionals to represent us well, but we are ultimately responsible for honest outcome. Furthermore, is there anything you are doing that would embarrass you and your family if printed as a newspaper headline? Indeed, integrity brings joy to heaven and security on earth. It is your guide for godly living.

"I put in charge of Jerusalem my brother Hanani, along with Hananiah the commander of the citadel, because he was a man of integrity and feared God more than most people do" (Nehemiah 7:2).

Moreover, the iniquity of the unfaithful destroys. The blessing of God is removed as it cannot be bought with bad behavior. Relationships are scarred and some severed over dishonest dealings. Overnight, poor judgment can soil and potentially destroy a hard-earned reputation. Pride acts as if integrity is only for others. It deceives itself and becomes a disgrace for its dishonest and duplicitous ways. Iniquity is an unfaithful guide.

So we ask ourselves, "How can I be a man or woman of integrity over the balance of my life?" There is simplicity about those who base their behavior on the principles in God's Word—nothing fancy, only faithful living in their daily routine. The grace of God governs their soul, the truth of God renews their mind, and accountability is an anchor for their actions. Honestly ask yourself, "Is integrity my faithful guide?"

"May integrity and uprightness protect me, because my hope is in you" (Psalm 25:21).

How can I better integrate integrity as a guide for my business dealings and behavior at home?

Related Readings: Genesis 20:4–7; Hosea 13:9; Matthew 7:13; Romans 7:9–12

REFLECTIONS

_____

_____

_____

_____

_____

52

CITIES FOR CHRIST

When the righteous prosper, the city rejoices;
when the wicked perish, there are shouts of joy.
Through the blessing of the upright a city is exalted.
Proverbs 11:10–11

How can we capture our cities for Christ? In the process, could our municipalities move toward institutions of integrity? Perhaps it starts with each of us who claims Jesus Christ as Savior. It is up to us to first get down on our knees and get down to business with our heavenly Father. The people of God make up the city of God. It is through our confession and repentance of sin that the city is set up for blessing from the Lord.

A city is not meant to be a passive party to the ways of wickedness. Daniel understood this and prayed this passionate prayer for his city: "O Lord, in keeping with all your righteous acts, turn away your anger and your wrath from Jerusalem, your city, your holy hill. Our sins and the iniquities of our fathers have made Jerusalem and your people an object of scorn to all those around us" (Daniel 9:16).

Furthermore, Christ influences cities by His church, upon the confession of His children: "He is Christ, Son of the living God." When we confess Christ with our words, backed by our life, we partner with the Holy Spirit in erecting the Lord's eternal edifice—His church. His dwelling is not captured by church buildings. His dwelling is in the hearts of men, women, boys, and girls who, empowered by His grace, give others the opportunity to hear the old, old story of Jesus' love for them. He is building His church for His glory.

Indeed, a city movement for Christ is birthed out of passionate prayer and brokenness. Jesus cried out for His city. "As he approached Jerusalem and saw the city, he wept over it" (Luke 19:41). Our tears become a tool of the Holy Spirit to transform us and others. There is healing as sorrow turns to joy. The early church rejoiced over this unleashing of the Lord's power. "So there was great joy in that city" (Acts 8:8).

Lastly, a city moved along by the Holy Spirit becomes a shining light of its Savior Jesus. He exalts the community on His hill of hope for all to see, believe, and be saved. Jesus says, "You are the light of the world. A city on a hill cannot be hidden" (Matthew 5:14). So we solemnly ask, "Have I claimed my city for Christ? Am I part of His movement?"

Whom can I invite to passionately pray with me over our city's movement toward God?

Related Readings: Genesis 41:38–42; Isaiah 16:5; Acts 13:44; 16:13–15

REFLECTIONS

_____

_____

_____

_____

_____

53

BENEFITS OF KINDNESS

A kindhearted woman gains respect, but ruthless men gain only wealth.
A kind man benefits himself, but a cruel man brings trouble on himself.
Proverbs 11:16–17

Kindness benefits everyone. It brings joy to the giver and peace to the receiver. The recipient reciprocates because respect is embedded in kindness. Kindheartedness facilitates respect as it treats others with dignity and honor. Even when offended or ostracized, a gracious heart takes the higher ground of humility and gentleness. It may not be liked, but it is respected. Kind actions attract the Almighty's approval.

What is kindness? At its core it is a reflection of Christ. It is what we expect of the Lord when we desire good things. Listen to the heart of this employee's prayer for his boss to experience God's kindness in marriage: "O LORD, God of my master Abraham, give me success today, and show kindness to my master Abraham" (Genesis 24:12). In the same way, your Savior shows you kindness in salvation and His severe mercy.

Furthermore, because of Christ's great kindness, you are compelled to compassionate action. Ruthless men and women use fear and intimidation to gain wealth and power, but considerate adults do not compromise their character for cash or influence. Indeed, God's great kindness grants us the favor we need.

"The LORD was with him [Joseph]; he showed him kindness and granted him favor in the eyes of the prison warden" (Genesis 39:21).

Who does not need kindness? The undeserving especially need your kindness as a reminder of God's lasting love and infinite forgiveness. Be kind to the unkind, and they will see what really rests in your heart of hearts. Your kindheartedness will lead others to your source in Jesus Christ. Here the kindness of the Lord leads to repentance.

"Or do you show contempt for the riches of his kindness, tolerance and patience, not realizing that God's kindness leads you toward repentance?" (Romans 2:4).

To whom can I extend kindness who has been unkind to me?

Related Readings: Joshua 2:12; Ruth 3:10; Acts 4:9; Ephesians 2:6–8

REFLECTIONS

_____

_____

_____

_____

_____

54

REFRESHERS ARE REFRESHED

A generous man will prosper; he who
refreshes others will himself be refreshed.
Proverbs 11:25

What does it mean to be refreshed? It is to be made fresh, to revive, enliven, invigorate, rejuvenate, energize, restore, recharge, or revitalize. A meager cup of lukewarm coffee comes alive with taste and satisfaction when mixed with freshly brewed beans. A lukewarm life is warmed and encouraged when refreshed with words of encouragement and acts of kindness. Everyone we meet becomes a candidate for refreshment.

Our faith cools down when Christ seems silent and circumstances continue to crumble, but a sincere prayer from a righteous friend restores and warms our confidence. Our hope feels deferred in the face of disappointment and rejection, but we are energized by the acceptance and love of a community of believers in Jesus. Hope loves company. Seek refreshment from your Savior and His followers. Be refreshed so you can refresh others.

"I will refresh the weary and satisfy the faint" (Jeremiah 31:25).

When your parched soul has been watered by dew from heaven, you can lead others to the Lord's watering hole. People are frantic from feeling robbed by insensitive institutions and greedy governments, but we can reconnect them to their generous God. Jesus gives us an abundant life to be shared with others who are absent of abundance. "I have come that they may have life, and that they may have it more abundantly" (John 10:10 NKJV).

Lastly, your refreshment reciprocates refreshment. When you refresh another financially, you are refreshed by faith and fulfillment. When you refresh another emotionally, you are refreshed by peace and contentment. When you refresh another spiritually, you are refreshed by the grace and love of God. Are you in need of refreshment? If so, receive Christ's full cup of joy. Drink often with the Lord so you can generously refresh friends.

"Taste and see that the LORD is good; blessed is the man who takes refuge in him" (Psalm 34:8).

How can I stay in a routine of refreshment so I in turn can refresh others?

Related Readings: Ruth 2:14; Psalm 41:1; Matthew 25:34–35; 2 Corinthians 9:6–7

REFLECTIONS

_____

_____

_____

_____

_____

55

FALSE TRUST

Whoever trusts in his riches will fall,
but the righteous will thrive like a green leaf.
Proverbs 11:28

Trust in stuff will cause you to stumble and eventually fall. Why? Why is money unfit for trust? It is unreliable because it cannot save us or bring us forgiveness, peace, and contentment. Money is an unemotional master that can trip you up if it becomes the basis for your security. It can be here today and gone tomorrow. Money moves around like a gypsy looking for the next place to live. Trust in riches falls from its focus on Christ.

Trust in riches causes some to fall from the faith because they equate wealth with success. However, you can be faithful to the Lord and thus be successful whether rich or poor. It may take our losing money to reveal our true motivations. Trust in riches is a recipe for false security, fear, and sadness.

"Cast but a glance at riches, and they are gone, for they will surely sprout wings and fly off to the sky like an eagle" (Proverbs 23:5).

However, the righteous understand the role of riches is to remind them of God's provision. The Bible says, "Moreover, when God gives any man wealth and possessions, and enables him to enjoy them, to accept his lot and be happy in his work—this is a gift of God" (Ecclesiastes 5:19). Are you struggling with the reduction of your wealth? Do you remember what really mattered when you were first married? Was it trust in the Lord, your spouse, and good health? The righteous thrive in trust and obedience to Christ.

Lastly, guard your good name during a financial crisis. Character is of much greater value than cash. The Bible says, "A good name is more desirable than great riches; to be esteemed is better than silver or gold" (Proverbs 22:1). This means you do not fear, and you follow through with your commitments. Faith grows in its giving during uncertain times. Am I thriving or surviving? Is my trust in gold or God?

Where does the Lord want me to aggressively give money, trusting in Him?

Related Readings: Deuteronomy 8:12–14; Job 31:24–25; Matthew 13:22; 1 Timothy 6:17

REFLECTIONS

_____

_____

_____

_____

56

NOBLE WIFE

A wife of noble character is her husband's crown,
but a disgraceful wife is like decay in his bones.
Proverbs 12:4

Why are certain wives attractive and others unattractive? Why do you enjoy the company of some but avoid the company of others? A wife of noble character is attractive because she aspires to obey almighty God. She is a joy to be around as she enjoys being in the presence of the Lord. Her first allegiance is to her Savior Jesus Christ, exhibited by her regal appearance and respectful responses. God has first place in her heart.

Her husband takes pride in her because she can be trusted in all household matters and financial management. By faith she follows her husband's leadership. She entrusts him under the authority of God to hold him accountable. A wife of noble character knows how to prayerfully ask challenging questions of her husband without usurping his leadership. She is strong and gracious, bold and beautiful, firm and friendly, faithful and loving.

"And now, my daughter, don't be afraid. I will do for you all you ask. All the people of my town know that you are a woman of noble character" (Ruth 3:11).

Her children are loved when they are unlovely and disciplined when they behave badly. They know their mom cares even when she gets carried away in her correction. A wife of noble character is a model of motherhood for her daughters and an example of one whom her sons should marry. She is wise to honor her husband in front of the children, especially when they disagree. Her character is a compass for the actions of her kids.

Lastly, a wife of noble character is not afraid to mentor and encourage other wives, not with a superior spirit but with an attitude of meekness and

SEEKING GOD IN THE PROVERBS

brokenness. She quickly admits to her past mistakes to save some young women from repeating the hurt and heartache. A student she remains even while she endeavors to teach and train. Wisdom is worn through her words with humility and grace. Indeed, a noble wife is a blessing to her husband.

"She is worth far more than rubies" (Proverbs 31:10).

How can I enjoy God's blessing of my husband and children?

Related Readings: Genesis 2:18–24; 1 Corinthians 11:7–11; 1 Timothy 5:2

REFLECTIONS

_____

_____

_____

_____

_____

57

UNPRETENTIOUS LIVING

Better to be a nobody and yet have a servant
than pretend to be somebody and have no food.
Proverbs 12:9

Unpretentious living is an invitation to down-to-earth interaction with others. Rest and relaxation attend to those who are true to themselves without acting like someone they are not. However, pretentious speech and behavior require extra energy to engage with their environment. Contentment is illusive, and intimacy is an illusion. I become the most stressful when I feel I have to live up to something or be someone I am not.

Moreover, when you are real, not fake, your friends feel the freedom to be the same. You give off energy instead of forever sucking it from others. I have to be honest and ask often, "Am I being myself, or am I trying to dress, talk, drive a certain car, or live in a high-status neighborhood, motivated by a need to be somebody I am not?" Pretense is birthed out of pride, but humility is the fruit of unpretentious living. Humility comes from Christ as He lives His life in and through you.

"Christ in you, the hope of glory" (Colossians 1:27).

Jesus is clear: "For everyone who exalts himself will be humbled, and he who humbles himself will be exalted" (Luke 14:11 NASB). In Christ you are somebody. High or low net worth, small or large home, new or used car, prestigious university or common college, in Him you are somebody. You are somebody to your Savior Jesus.

Out of your simple faith and modesty the Lord takes center stage of your life. Humility positions you to point people to heaven. Therefore, keep your life unencumbered so people can see your Savior shine forth. Ask yourself,

SEEKING GOD IN THE PROVERBS

"Whom am I trying to impress, people I really do not know or the Lover of my soul, Jesus?"

"Those who want to make a good impression outwardly are trying to compel you to be circumcised. The only reason they do this is to avoid being persecuted for the cross of Christ" (Galatians 6:12).

How can I be more authentic and open with my spouse, children, and work associates?

Related Readings: 1 Samuel 16:7; Proverbs 13:7; Romans 2:28; 1 Peter 3:3

REFLECTIONS

_____

_____

_____

_____

_____

58

ROUTINE WORK

He who works his land will have abundant food,
but he who chases fantasies lacks judgment.
Proverbs 12:11

Routine work may not be sexy, but it is necessary. It is necessary to meet our needs and the needs of those who depend on us. The same work, day in and day out, can seem simple and even boring, but it is a test of our faithfulness. Will I continue to faithfully carry out uncomplicated responsibilities, even when my attention span is suffering? If so, this is God's path to blessing. "Steady plodding brings prosperity" (Proverbs 21:5 LB).

The contrast to routine work is chasing after phantom deals that are figments of our imagination. Be careful not to be led astray by fantasies that lead nowhere. It is false faith to think a gimmick or some conniving circumstance can replace hard work. Wisdom stops chasing after the next scheme and sticks instead to the certainty of available work. What does your spouse say is the smart thing to do? Give your spouse all the facts, and listen.

Furthermore, work is easily carried out when everything is going well and there are no indicators of job loss or an increase in responsibility with less pay. However, it is during these uncertain times that Christ followers can step up and set the example. Your attitude of hope and hard work is a testimony of trust in the Lord. Stay engaged in executing your tasks with excellence, and you will inspire others in their labor of love.

Lastly, see routine work as your worship of the Lord. He is blessing your faithfulness to follow through with the smallest of details. Are you content to serve Christ in your current career? Work is your way to show the world your Savior. Excellence in what you do attracts attention to what almighty God can do. He is your audience of one in your routine work.

"Whatever you do, work at it with all your heart, as working for the Lord, not for men, since you know that you will receive an inheritance from the Lord as a reward. It is the Lord Christ you are serving" (Colossians 3:23–24).

Lord, in what ways can I reflect You in my everyday responsibilities at work?

Related Readings: Genesis 2:15; 1 Kings 19:19; Romans 12:11; 1 Timothy 4:11–12

REFLECTIONS

_____

_____

_____

_____

_____

59

PATIENT FORGIVENESS

A fool shows his annoyance at once, but a prudent man overlooks an insult.
Proverbs 12:16

Fools are forever flailing away at an offense, while a prudent man or woman is patient to forgive. A fool is easily provoked to anger, always looking for an argument to win. He or she is combative with uncompassionate concern. However, prudence is careful in its response, not willing to be reckless but just to be right. Wisdom employs forethought and prayer so that it answers with an attitude of respect. Prudence invokes patience.

Do you buckle under pressure and say things you later regret? It is better to keep quiet and cool down than to vent venomous words in the flesh. Make this a goal when disciplining your children. Avoid anger as the instructor of your punishment. We tend to speak harshly and act unreasonably when driven by anger. Wait prayerfully for twenty-four hours; then revisit the infraction with your child. Use cool correction.

"They sent word to Joseph, saying, 'Your father left these instructions before he died: "This is what you are to say to Joseph: I ask you to forgive your brothers the sins and the wrongs they committed in treating you so badly." Now please forgive the sins of the servants of the God of your father.' When their message came to him, Joseph wept" (Genesis 50:16–17).

Bridle your tongue by God's grace. The Bible says, "If anyone considers himself religious and yet does not keep a tight rein on his tongue, he deceives himself and his religion is worthless" (James 1:26). Your words can grieve another or give hope. They can hurt or heal. Therefore, submit to the Holy Spirit's control of your conversations.

Lastly, you are blessed if you are insulted for Christ sake. "Blessed are you when people insult you, persecute you and falsely say all kinds of evil against you because of me" (Matthew 5:11). Reward awaits those rejected for right-eousness sake. Have you died to the right to be right? Do you hold a grudge or have to get even? In Christ we are dead to sin, and the dead are not insulted.

"In the same way, count yourselves dead to sin but alive to God in Christ Jesus" (Romans 6:11).

Whom do I need to patiently forgive for Christ's sake?

Related Readings: 1 Samuel 20:30–34; Esther 3:5; Matthew 27:39–40; James 1:19

REFLECTIONS

_____

_____

_____

_____

_____

60

DILIGENCE RULES

Diligent hands will rule, but laziness ends in slave labor.
Proverbs 12:24

How hard do you work, or do you hardly work? God said to Adam, "Cursed is the ground because of you; through painful toil you will eat of it all the days of your life. By the sweat of your brow you will eat your food" (Genesis 3:17, 19). And He explained to Moses, "Six days you shall labor and do all your work, but the seventh day is a Sabbath to the LORD your God. On it you shall not do any work" (Exodus 20:9–10).

Has our culture become accustomed to receiving good things without great effort? Who is entitled to influence without being industrious? Perhaps there is a dearth of diligence that has depressed people and economies. Laziness leads to the control of others, while honest labor is given opportunities and advancement. Do not despair in your diligence for you are set for success. Mind your business meticulously, and you will enjoy the business.

"Now the man Jeroboam was a valiant warrior, and when Solomon saw that the young man was industrious, he appointed him over all the forced labor of the house of Joseph" (1 Kings 11:28 NASB).

Indeed, intense industry leads to preferment. Your faithfulness to your work is not going unnoticed. Your diligence is a distinctive that separates you from the average or lazy laborer. Security comes with this level of service. Promotion follows performance that produces the right results the right way. Be an industrious example others seek to emulate.

Lastly, the Lord blesses hands that are hard at work. He smiles when He sees your service exceeds expectations. You go the extra mile to make sure others are cared for as you would like to be treated. Because of your thoroughness on the job and your integrity in its execution, God knows you can be trusted with more.

"The elders who direct the affairs of the church well are worthy of double honor, especially those whose work is preaching and teaching" (1 Timothy 5:17).

Lord, what task do You desire that I diligently complete before beginning another?

Related Readings: 1 Kings 12:20; Proverbs 10:4; Romans 12:8;
1 Timothy 4:15

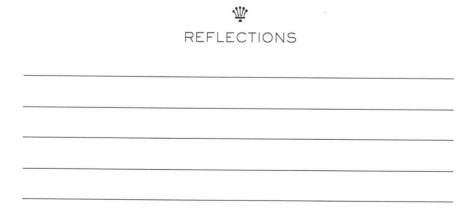

REFLECTIONS

61

RIGHTEOUS HATRED

The righteous hate what is false,
but the wicked bring shame and disgrace.
Proverbs 13:5

There is a righteous hatred that rejects what is false. It might be false words, bogus behavior, a counterfeit countenance, a phony friendship, or deceptive dealings. The discernment of the Spirit-filled believer rises up to defend integrity. You cannot sit still to shenanigans when you know an agreed-upon code of ethics has been violated.

So how are we to respond to lies and liars? We first look in the mirror, making sure we are honest in our dealings and accurate with our words. Jesus said, "How can you say to your brother, 'Let me take the speck out of your eye,' when all the time there is a plank in your own eye?" (Matthew 7:4). I am required to remove all self-deception before I can clearly see sin in my brother. Self-evaluation precedes confronting false conduct.

Furthermore, our heavenly Father expresses holy hatred over what is false. "The LORD hates ... haughty eyes, a lying tongue ... a heart that devises wicked schemes" (Proverbs 6:16–18). Because the Almighty abhors artificial acts, we must ask ourselves, "Do I take sin seriously, or do I casually flirt with it?" Loose lips lead to lies and deceit that bring shame and embarrassment. Avoid lies and liars, and you will live in peaceful content.

"But now I am writing to you that you must not associate with anyone who claims to be a brother or sister but is sexually immoral or greedy, an idolater or slanderer, a drunkard or swindler. Do not even eat with such people" (1 Corinthians 5:11).

Lastly, in your business, ministry, and testimony, remove all appearance of fraud and falsehood. Free yourself from image management with full disclosure and transparency. Create a culture that exposes any hint of conflict of interest. Lies examined under light melt away. Hate dishonesty; reward honesty. Honesty is the only policy for the people of God.

"Therefore each of you must put off falsehood and speak truthfully to his neighbor, for we are all members of one body" (Ephesians 4:25).

What areas of my life and work need to grow in honesty and forthrightness?

Related Readings: Judges 16:11; Psalm 119:163; Colossians 3:9; Revelation 21:8

REFLECTIONS

_____

_____

_____

_____

_____

62

RIGHTEOUS LIGHT

The light of the righteous shines brightly,
but the lamp of the wicked is snuffed out.
Proverbs 13:9

Righteousness shines the brightest when dimming days become the darkest. We are called and compelled as Christians to glow for God during gloomy times. Are you caught up in our culture's chaos, or do you see a chance to burn brightly for Jesus? Hard times can harden our hearts or humble them, but it is a broken heart that burns the brightest.

Jesus said, "In the same way, let your light shine before men, that they may see your good deeds and praise your Father in heaven" (Matthew 5:16). Light left unattended extinguishes, but light exposed to the air of almighty God's love illuminates. Difficult days demand dependency on the Lord; so in fact, your acts of service are fueled by faith. If you panic instead of praying, you will miss out on opportunities to love others.

"We ought always to thank God for you, brothers and sisters, and rightly so, because your faith is growing more and more, and the love all of you have for one another is increasing" (2 Thessalonians 1:3).

I often ask, "In my uncertainty, am I more worried about my stuff or the window of opportunity to serve others?" It may mean inviting someone to live in my home for a season, paying mortgage payments for three months for a friend, volunteering at a local shelter, or increasing my gifts to the church. Righteous light longs to love liberally.

Christ in us invites others to know Him, "For God, who said, 'Let light shine out of darkness,' made his light shine in our hearts to give us the light of the knowledge of the glory of God in the face of Christ" (2 Corinthians 4:6). Perhaps you invite some neighbors over for a six-week Bible study on money or marriage and watch what God does.

"Do everything without complaining or arguing, so that you may become blameless and pure, children of God without fault in a crooked and depraved generation, in which you shine like stars in the universe" (Philippians 2:14–15).

Where can I bring the light of Christ's love to someone's dark circumstance?

Related Readings: Job 18:5–6; Isaiah 50:10–11; Luke 11:36; Revelation 21:23

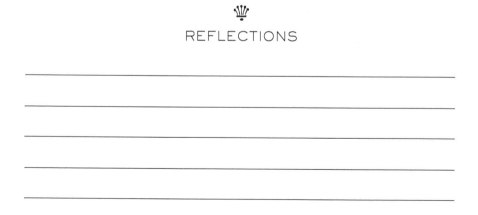

REFLECTIONS

_____

_____

_____

_____

_____

63

DOLLAR COST AVERAGING

Dishonest money dwindles away,
but he who gathers money little by little makes it grow.
Proverbs 13:11

Is there a method to your money management? Do you have a process in place to steadily save over time? If not, it is never too late to set up a system for saving. Some of us struggle with this because we bet on big returns, only to suffer loss. Steadily saving is not sexy but secure. Finances can be an elusive enemy or a friend who has our back.

Get-rich-quick schemes only feed greed. In God's economy, it is those who diligently deposit smaller amounts in a secure place who reap rewards. It is wise wealth that makes the first ten percent of its income a gift offering in the form of a tithe to the heavenly Father and the second ten percent an investment in the future. Money obtained by vanity is spent on vanity, but money gained by hard work and honesty is retained for growth.

"Unless the LORD builds the house, the builders labor in vain. Unless the LORD watches over the city, the guards stand watch in vain. In vain you rise early and stay up late, ?toiling for food to eat—for he grants sleep to those he loves" (Psalm 127:1–2).

It does take discipline not to spend all our earnings in an instant. Commercials and our obligation as consumers exploit our emotions. Culture sucks us in to spend not all we have but more than we have; so be on guard with a simple system for savings. For example, set up an automatic draft from each paycheck that goes straight into a savings account. Preserve this cash; one day your financial fruit tree will become an orchard.

Lastly, look to the Lord as your provider, seeing yourself as a steward of His stuff. The management of your Master's money requires saving. God's desire is growth in your financial security so you are free to give more and serve others. So we ask ourselves, "Am I frivolously spending just for today, or am I disciplined each day to deposit a dollar toward tomorrow?"

"The plans of the diligent lead to profit as surely as haste leads to poverty" (Proverbs 21:5).

Lord, how would you have me manage Your money today in preparation for tomorrow?

Related Readings: Psalm 128:2; Jeremiah 17:11; Ephesians 4:28; James 5:1–5

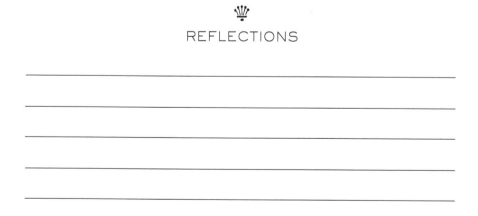

REFLECTIONS

_____

_____

_____

_____

_____

64

WISDOM IS LEARNED

The proverbs of Solomon son of David, king of Israel: for gaining
wisdom and instruction; for understanding words of insight; for receiving
instruction in prudent behavior, doing what is right and just and fair.
Proverbs 1:1-3

There is a definite educational element to wisdom. It does not
happen in a spiritual vacuum or without intellectual effort. Those who excel in
becoming wise learn how to educate themselves in the ways of wisdom. They
read the Bible and other writings that define wisdom, with a filter of faith in
God. There are wise sayings outside of Holy Writ, but beyond the context of
Christ, wisdom drifts into a cheap imitation in worldly wisdom.

Therefore, for wisdom to be the most meaningful, it must incubate and grow in
a teachable and humble heart. A seed of corn does not germinate on the surface of hard soil. In a similar ecosystem, seeds of wisdom bring life and insight
to a heart moistened by heaven's righteous rain. Lifetime learners understand
the need to always gain wisdom. Moses, upon a foundation of faith, was educated in wisdom in preparation to become one of God's chosen leaders.

"Moses was educated in all the wisdom of the Egyptians and was powerful in
speech and action" (Acts 7:22).

However, it is from an unselfish motivation and a humble attitude that the
Lord's wisdom is able to transform a life. Wisdom is not for personal gain but
for the propagation of almighty God's agenda. A once wise man becomes a
fool when he uses divine insight for individual advantage instead of the good
of the group. What is God teaching you? How are you growing wise in your
parenting, marriage, and decision-making skills?

Educators in wisdom are all around. Pray for your pastor to sit at the feet of
Jesus in prayer so his mind might be molded by the Holy Spirit's insights and
instruction. Look for wisdom from faithful saints who penned timeless words,

while they worked through their suffering and triumphs as disciples of Jesus. Wisdom comes from PhDs, village preachers, and everyone in between. Wisdom abounds where the wise are found. Remember—the less you talk, the more wisdom you gain, as you listen to learn.

"Let the wise listen and add to their learning, and let the discerning get guidance" (Proverbs 1:5).

So be a student of your Savior Jesus' wisdom, and you will never lack for knowledge. Wisdom is what attracts your children and grandchildren to want to be with you. The wise age well—like a robust wine—while fools flounder in insecure ignorance. Wise Christians are continually educated in wisdom so that they can prayerfully educate others.

"His [Christ's] intent was that now, through the church, the manifold wisdom of God should be made known" (Ephesians 3:10).

Whom can I learn from and gain a heart of godly wisdom?

Related Readings: Proverbs 11:2; Jeremiah 49:7; Luke 2:52; Ephesians 1:8

REFLECTIONS

_____

_____

_____

_____

_____

65

LOVE DISCIPLINES

He who spares the rod hates his son,
but he who loves him is careful to discipline him.
Proverbs 13:24

Love carefully disciplines; apathy silently ignores. Love looks for ways to instruct and improve, while busyness has no time for a tender touch of truth. Do you take the time to discipline your children? Do your offspring encounter your rebuke along with your encouragement? Because we love them, we correct their attitudes and challenge them to better behavior. Rules restrain them from reacting foolishly or in the flesh.

How can our children learn to make wise decisions if we do not discipline them to love and obey God? Like a skilled artist with a warm lump of clay, our children are moldable, and their character is pliable in Christ's hands. We seek consistency in our own character so we have the moral authority and respect to lead them. Your children's first impression of the Lord is their father and mother; so be an authority who reveals His love.

"The living, the living—they praise you, as I am doing today; parents tell their children about your faithfulness" (Isaiah 38:19).

The branch of a tree is easily bent when it is tender; so start when they are young with yielding to Christ's lordship. "Train a child in the way he should go, and when he is old he will not turn from it" (Proverbs 22:6). Foolishness flees from faith and the prayerful punishment of loving parents. "Folly is bound up in the heart of a child, but the rod of discipline will drive it far from him" (Proverbs 22:15). Discipline leads to freedom.

You may lament the need for respect from your son or daughter. It is your consistent concern for your children's character growth that invites their respect. "Fathers ... disciplined us and we respected them for it" (Hebrews 12:9). Moreover, loving parents honestly inquire, "How do I respond to the Lord's discipline?" My example of growth from my heavenly Father's discipline makes me an earthly father worth following.

"For whom the LORD loves He reproves, Even as a father corrects the son in whom he delights" (Proverbs 3:12 NASB).

What area of my child's growth requires me to be more consistent in discipline?

Related Readings: Proverbs 23:13–14; 29:15–17; Hebrews 12:6–8; Ephesians 6:4

REFLECTIONS

_____

_____

_____

_____

_____

66

EMPTY NEST

Where there are no oxen, the manager is empty,
but from the strength of an ox comes an abundant harvest.
Proverbs 14:4

How do you feel since your home has emptied of children? Mad, sad, glad, lonely, without purpose, or freed up may all be legitimate emotions you are processing. You have raised them well, and now they are on their own. You are proud of them, but you miss them. They call from college (especially daughters), but it is not the same. It is not easy to export your babies into adulthood; however, this is their faith walk to really know God.

We raise them the best we know how with love, discipline, and belief in Jesus Christ. Sometimes they frustrate us by not cleaning their crib (room). Like an animal in a barn, they can be messy and smelly. There are days you want a little peace and quiet because they are angry and loud when fighting with their siblings. But the empty nest is void of noise. The kids are nowhere to be found; so enjoy them while you can.

"Train up a child in the way he should go, And when he is old he will not depart from it" (Proverbs 22:6 NKJV).

You send them off to grow up and gain a heart of gratitude. By God's grace they will visit with a new sense of appreciation and maturity. Distance causes friendship with your adult child to grow, not be taken for granted. It is harder to keep up and communicate, but in some ways it is more gratifying. You prepared them to leave so they can cleave to the one the Lord has for them in marriage. Our empty nest is a test of trust in God's plan.

Lastly, engage with your spouse in your empty nest. Do you feel like you have drifted apart over the years? If so, be intentional to regain the intense intimacy with your best friend. Make these days of marriage your best; believe the Lord has given you your lover to grow old together. Anticipate the gift of grandkids, as they will keep you busy and lively. The empty nest is a season to enjoy the fruit of your family.

"A good man leaves an inheritance for his children's children" (Proverbs 13:22).

Lord, how can I best use the season of life I am in for Your kingdom purposes?

Related Readings: Genesis 7:1; Proverbs 31:15; Matthew 19:5; Acts 10:2

REFLECTIONS

_____

_____

_____

_____

_____

67

SELF-DECEPTION

There is a way that seems right to a man,
but in the end it leads to death.
Proverbs 14:12

Self-deception is the worst kind of dishonesty because it is so convincing. Subtly it convenes our mind and emotions to ally around a lie. For example, self-deception whispers into the ear of our heart, "You are so smart and capable," but it forgets to include Christ's influence in its instruction. Then we wander down a prayerless path, forged in our own strength, only to discover we missed God's best by a mile.

In reality, we are only as prosperous as our Lord allows. He makes our path straight and successful as He defines success. "I guide you in the way of wisdom and lead you along straight paths" (Proverbs 4:11). To which voice do you adhere—your own or your Savior's? Perhaps His plan is for you to make less money and have more family time. Maybe you turn down this promotion and trust Him for a better one in a different season.

"The pride of your heart has deceived you" (Obadiah 1:3).

We can talk ourselves into anything, especially as it relates to money. I can easily justify a new house, car, kitchen, furniture, floors, or grill. But do I really need to upgrade or just repair what I have? How can the Lord trust me with something newer if I have not been a good steward of what He has already given me? Trustworthy people can be trusted with more, but the distrusting lose opportunities. Thus manage well your present possessions.

Self-deceivers are self-destroyers; so avoid self-delusion by being accountable. Give others permission to ask you uncomfortable, even hard, questions. Better to be embarrassed sooner than humiliated later. Humility invites the inspection of loving friends into our lives. You do much better when others provide loving accountability.

"The heart is hopelessly dark and deceitful, a puzzle that no one can figure out. But I, God, search the heart and examine the mind. I get to the heart of the human. I get to the root of things. I treat them as they really are, not as they pretend to be" (Jeremiah 17:9 MSG).

Am I transparent with my money and motives? What do God and godly advisors think?

Related Readings: Psalm 1:6; Isaiah 59:8; Matthew 7:13–14; Galatians 6:3

REFLECTIONS

_____

_____

_____

_____

_____

68

KIND TO THE NEEDY

He who despises his neighbor sins,
but blessed is he who is kind to the needy.
Proverbs 14:21

The needy have unmet needs that cripple their ability to live life to its fullest. It may be the need for food, clothing, or a place to live. They may need a job, a car, or an opportunity to get ahead. The needy may be lost in their sins without Christ, which is the greatest of needs. Wherever their point of need lies is our obligation to kindly care for them. "Give to the poor, and you will have treasure in heaven" (Matthew 19:21).

Evidence of our following Jesus is shown by our caring concern for the poor. Our kindness may require us to give up something so that another can gain something. Perhaps there is a fun trip you give up so a poor person can enjoy food for a month. What financial expenditure can you put on pause? Do you know someone who could benefit from a car repair or a mortgage payment? Sacrifice solicits most when the need of others is highest.

"Whoever oppresses the poor shows contempt for their Maker, but whoever is kind to the needy honors God" (Proverbs 14:31).

Furthermore, the best motivation for reaching out is kindness of heart, not guilt of mind. It is a kind word that lifts another person's spirit. It is a generous gratuity to a diligent server. It is a gentle response to a demanding spirit. The needy are all around us, especially during economic downturns. Maybe there is a neighbor who is out of work whom you can invite into your home to dinner and for encouragement. Kindness is a culprit of compassion and care.

Lastly, look out for the needy because of the Lord's great love toward you. Kindness asks, "Where would I be without God's grace? Where in my life can

I extend His grace, love, and mercy?" Blessings await those who give and receive kindness. We are all needy, some more than others, but our provider is the same—Jesus Christ.

"Because of the LORD'S great love we are not consumed, for his compassions never fail" (Lamentations 3:22).

Who in my life is in need whom I can show kindness to in Jesus' name?

Related Readings: Deuteronomy 15:4; Isaiah 58:7–12; Luke 6:30–36; 1 John 3:17–22

REFLECTIONS

_____

_____

_____

_____

_____

69

SUBMISSION SOLICITS SECURITY

He who fears the LORD has a secure fortress,
and for his children it will be a refuge.
Proverbs 14:26

Submission is a friend of the secure. Submitting to authority is the secret to securing peace of mind and protection. It is when we demand our own way and avoid authority that we expose ourselves to the enemy and his devices. "Submit yourselves, then, to God. Resist the devil, and he will flee from you" (James 4:7). Submission is a shield.

So submission begins by fearing the Lord. It is an attitude of humility, not pride; trust, not worry; respect, not lip service; and obedience, not foolishness. Our heart bows down in worship while our head learns how to love and obey. Under the Almighty's authority, we are sheltered by His great grace. "He who dwells in the shelter of the Most High will rest in the shadow of the Almighty" (Psalm 91:1). Fear of God is where freedom is found.

"The midwives, however, feared God and did not do what the king of Egypt had told them to do; they let the boys live" (Exodus 1:17).

Furthermore, our model of submission to our Savior is a template for our children, peers, and followers to apply. However, if they see us skirt around submission, they may secretly seek exceptions. Rebellion comes to roost when we become selective in our obedience. What happens when your boss is unreasonable? Do you still submit to his authority? Yes, and let your excellent work become a testimony of trust in the Lord.

Lastly, what about a wife's submission to her husband? You submit to him and pray for him to understand his accountability to God because he is account-able. A husband who comes under Christ's authority showers his bride with security, a gift she cherishes deeply. Therefore, build a firm fortress of faith. Secure couples submit first to God.

"Submit to God and be at peace with him; in this way prosperity will come to you" (Job 22:21).

Am I under the authority of God and man? Does my submission result in service to others?

Related Readings: Genesis 16:9; 2 Chronicles 30:8; Romans 13:1–5; Ephesians 5:21–24

REFLECTIONS

_____

_____

_____

_____

_____

70

A NATION EXALTED

Righteousness exalts a nation, but sin is a disgrace to any people.
Proverbs 14:34

What makes a nation, any nation, great? It's goodness is what God blesses. Righteousness is the lever the Lord uses to lift up a nation as an example for other nations to follow. However, like people a nation can fall from God's grace. His blessing is removed when a haughty country shows no remorse for sin and even sanctions its use. A blessed nation will cease to be great when it forgets where it came from by jettisoning Jesus.

It is when a nation is hurting that it needs healing most. The nation of Israel experienced this. "If my people, who are called by my name, will humble themselves and pray and seek my face and turn from their wicked ways, then will I hear from heaven and will forgive their sin and will heal their land" (2 Chronicles 7:14). Have we drifted as a nation to not needing God? Has our sin found us out? Are we reaping what we have sown?

"In that day you will say: 'Give praise to the LORD, proclaim his name; make known among the nations what he has done, and proclaim that his name is exalted'" (Isaiah 12:4).

The good news is that an exalted nation does not have people sneaking out but instead sneaking in. Peoples of the world clamor to a country Christ has blessed. The best and the brightest are drawn like a moth to a light to live somewhere they can chase their dreams. It is out of its goodness that a nation becomes a magnet for mankind. Righteousness reposes in the heart of a great nation, supporting virtue and suppressing vice.

Lastly, a crippled country can come back, but not without consequences. It starts with individuals repenting and taking responsibility for their actions. "How can I come clean with Christ?" "Have I been financially irresponsible?" "Has greed governed my giving?" "Has fear frozen my faith?" "Have comfort and ease become my idol?" The Lord exalts a nation that stays on its knees in dependence and awe of almighty God.

"He has declared that he will set you in praise, fame and honor high above all the nations he has made and that you will be a people holy to the LORD your God, as he promised" (Deuteronomy 26:19).

God, what do I need to do in order for You to again trust our nation with greatness?

Related Readings: Proverbs 11:11; Jeremiah 22:2–25; Matthew 12:21; Romans 16:25–27

REFLECTIONS

A GENTLE ANSWER

A gentle answer turns away wrath, but a harsh word stirs up anger.
Proverbs 15:1

A gentle answer is not easy to come by in stressful situations.
Financial pressures tend to push buttons that arouse my flesh, and in my own strength I say things I later regret. It is hard not to be harsh when the weight of the world weighs us down or when we feel misunderstood or underappreciated. Indeed, this is when the gentleness of Jesus can replace our juvenile gestures. "Take my yoke upon you and learn from me, for I am gentle and humble in heart, and you will find rest for your souls" (Matthew 11:29).

Harshness seems to hibernate in a heavy heart, awakening when it feels violated or disturbed. However, by God's grace, a soft reply allows reason to run its course rather than passionate words that provoke insult. Emotion is kept in check by calm communication that promotes peace and understanding. Consider reaching out patiently.

"An anxious heart weighs a man down, but a kind word cheers him up" (Proverbs 12:25).

If you find yourself in a heated argument, take a deep breath and pray together. It is hard to remain angry when you are on your knees confessing sin and sorrow to your Savior Jesus. Take the lead to apologize and ask forgiveness. Humility disarms explosive conversations and brings back the calm of Christ. Remind each other of Jesus' words, "So in everything, do to others what you would have them do to you" (Matthew 7:12).

Lastly, a gentle word from God lowers your blood pressure and gives you a peaceful perspective. Listen to the Lord before you lash out, and His Spirit will restrain you from stupid stunts. The work of the Holy Spirit in your heart moves you from harshness to holiness. Pray, "Lord, forgive me and fill me." It is the fullness of the Spirit that frees you from the foul flesh. As a Spirit-filled believer, you smell sweet to your Savior Jesus and all who love Him.

"But the fruit of the Spirit is love, joy, peace, patience, kindness, goodness, faithfulness, gentleness and self-control" (Galatians 5:22–23).

Lord, my heart desires a daily surrender and refreshing of Your life-giving Spirit.

Related Readings: 1 Kings 9:11–13; Proverbs 25:15; Matthew 12:36–37; Colossians 3:12

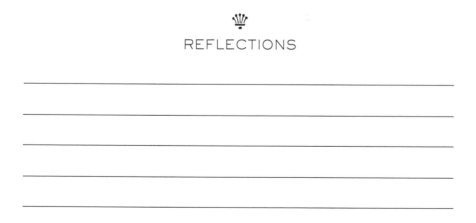

REFLECTIONS

72

PURSUE RIGHTEOUSNESS

The LORD detests the way of the wicked
but he loves those who pursue righteousness.
Proverbs 15:9

What does it mean to pursue righteousness? We pursue happiness. We pursue financial security. We pursue a husband or wife for marriage, but what is the pursuit of righteousness? It is a standard of behavior that is morally right or justifiable as God defines right. We pursue righteousness when we determine to understand what the Scripture outlines as right, integrating it into our behavior. It is intentional living.

The pursuit of righteousness begins with the pursuit of God, for He is the Righteous One. He detests the way of the wicked but loves those who pursue righteousness. He loves those who pursue Him for righteousness sake. So we seek Him because we need Him to transform us into the likeness of His Son Jesus. We become like what we pursue.

"The Righteous One takes note of the house of the wicked and brings the wicked to ruin" (Proverbs 21:12).

It is the path of the righteous He makes smooth, not without bumps along the way but with clear direction for living. Perhaps you ask, "How do I know God's will for school, marriage, or work?" Pursue righteousness, and He will direct your steps. Do not worry and fret over step fourteen; instead, by faith focus on the next step. "The path of the righteous is level; O upright One, you make the way of the righteous smooth" (Isaiah 26:7).

Without your Lord and Savior Jesus, your "righteous acts are like filthy rags" (Isaiah 64:6). Indeed, it is not what you do for Jesus but the work of His Spirit in and through you to produce the fruit of righteousness. Remain in Him, and

SEEKING GOD IN THE PROVERBS

He will make you righteous—not holier-than-thou, but humble and loving. Your pursuits are what you become; thus wise are you and loved by the Lord when you pursue righteousness.

"Abide in Me, and I in you. As the branch cannot bear fruit of itself, unless it abides in the vine, neither can you, unless you abide in Me" (John 15:4 NKJV).

Am I pursuing righteousness by abiding in Christ?

Related Readings: 1 Chronicles 29:17; Psalm 1:6; 1 Timothy 6:11; 2 Timothy 2:22

REFLECTIONS

_____

_____

_____

_____

_____

73

A HAPPY HEART

A happy heart makes the face cheerful, but heartache crushes the spirit.
Proverbs 15:13

A happy heart aligns with heaven's perspective. It is committed to something much broader and nobler than current circumstances. A heart of delight is not in denial about difficulties, nor is it irresponsible regarding raw reality; it takes its cheer from Christ. People can encourage us, but it is Jesus who provides eternal encouragement. "Do not let your hearts be troubled. Trust in God; trust also in me" (John 14:1).

A cheerful face does not mean a heart is not hurting. You may very well be suffering painful rejection from divorce, job loss, or missed opportunity. However, the aching of a hopeful heart is accompanied by assurance anchored in almighty God. Hurt need not exclude happiness. Go to Jesus for affirmation, and He will make your heart whole and happy.

"Even in laughter the heart may ache, and joy may end in grief" (Proverbs 14:13).

Sometimes your spirit is crushed in the moment you receive information you do not completely understand. Someone may treat you disrespectfully. You later learn of the deep wounds that person is carrying without Christ. Maybe a team member who is a loyal friend and confidant is moving on. You feel betrayed and alone. Use this loss to lead you toward the Lord's love and healing. Our loss is God's gain in governing our hearts.

The disciples felt loss and sorrow before the cross. Jesus discerned this and said, "Because I have said these things, you are filled with grief. But I tell you the truth: It is for your good that I am going away. Unless I go away, the

Counselor will not come to you; but if I go, I will send him to you" (John 16:6–7). He is the emissary of eternal happiness. A happy heart is full of faith in the Lord. Peer into the face of Christ, and you will go away with a cheerful countenance. Follow His commands, and find joy.

"The precepts of the LORD are right, giving joy to the heart. The commands of the LORD are radiant, giving light to the eyes" (Psalm 19:8).

Is my heart full of the Holy Spirit's control; am I happy and content in Christ?

Related Readings: Nehemiah 2:2; Proverbs 12:25; Acts 27:25–36; 2 Corinthians 2:7

REFLECTIONS

_____

_____

_____

_____

_____

74

PATIENCE CALMS DOWN

A hot-tempered man stirs up dissension, but a patient man calms a quarrel.
Proverbs 15:18

Anger stirs up; patience calms down. Anger has an axe to grind; patience smooths over offenses. Anger reacts in the moment; patience refrains to process. Anger rejects; patience accepts. Anger gets revenge; patience forgives. The goal of anger is to win the quarrel. The goal of patience is to win the relationship. "Patient persistence pierces through indifference; gentle speech breaks down rigid defenses" (Proverbs 25:15 MSG).

My anger sometimes gets the best of me, and I say things I later regret. This is when I can choose to humble myself and ask forgiveness from my offenders or ignore injury and risk lingering hurt. Over time, unresolved anger compounds into a crisis of trust, as anger invites insecurity. People avoid fools who are "an argument" waiting to happen.

"It is to a man's honor to avoid strife, but every fool is quick to quarrel" (Proverbs 20:3).

Patience is a peacemaker. It carries buckets of words and, like water, douses the flames of fury and rage. Patience is a prince of peace, a convener of calm conversations. Patience perceives the bigger picture of the Lord's work and is not caught up in petty, emotional outbursts. Because "love is patient" (1 Corinthians 13:4), it is a matter of loving people through their misfortune or misunderstanding. Love conquers and then calms.

Lastly, the Lord provides patience in prayer. When you silently wait before Him, He waits with you. It is a lesson in lingering before the Lord and listening to His intimate instructions. Prayer leads me to ponder, "Will I trust God and wait patiently, or will I prove my point in pride?" Christ calms me so I can patiently create a calm culture.

"Be still in the presence of the LORD, and wait patiently for him to act. Don't worry about evil people who prosper or fret about their wicked schemes" (Psalm 37:7 NLT).

Lord, how can I replace selfish anger with patient forgiveness and love?

Related Readings: Psalm 140:2; Ecclesiastes 10:4; Matthew 5:9; 1 Timothy 1:16

REFLECTIONS

_____

_____

_____

_____

_____

75

WISE PLANNING

Plans fail for lack of counsel, but with many advisers they succeed.
Proverbs 15:22

Wise planning is collaborative in nature as it understands the wisdom found in diverse perspectives. It is not intimidated by input but invites it. Otherwise, we are limited by our own ideas, experience, and intellect. Wise planning is a way to assure success and minimize risk. We are presumptuous and irresponsible not to pay the price of planning. Even King David validated the plan with the people:

"The plan seemed right both to the king and to the whole assembly" (2 Chronicles 30:4).

First of all, prayerfully seek God's plan. Prayerful planning produces the best results. Schedule prayer time with your team, and then get up off your knees to plan. Plans marinated in prayer are seasoned with success. Seek the Lord, and He will show you the wisest way. A prayerful plan is not limited by man but has infinite upside in God's hand.

"'All this,' David said, 'I have in writing from the hand of the LORD upon me, and he gave me understanding in all the details of the plan'" (1 Chronicles 28:19).

The Lord has the best plan; so prayerfully understand His ways, and you will save time and money avoiding mistakes. "'For I know the plans I have for you,' declares the LORD, 'plans to prosper you and not to harm you, plans to give you hope and a future'" (Jeremiah 29:11). Your primary counselor is Christ; so go to Him often for insight. Do not be dismayed if your plan is delayed. God's timing reaps radical results that last.

Lastly, look for validation from godly advisors beginning with your spouse and those who know you well. Also, listen to the advice you would give someone in a similar situation. You will not regret following the same planning process you prescribe for others. Wise planning works with, not against, the Spirit's leadership to get God-glorified results.

"Many are the plans in a man's heart, but it is the LORD'S purpose that prevails" (Proverbs 19:21).

Do I practice what I preach, following a prayerful planning process, or do I make exceptions and seek shortcuts?

Related Readings: Psalm 33:11; Isaiah 25:1; Romans 1:13; Hebrews 11:40

REFLECTIONS

_____

_____

_____

_____

_____

76

PURE THOUGHTS

The LORD detests the thoughts of the wicked,
but those of the pure are pleasing to him.
Proverbs 15:26

Pure thoughts are pleasing to the Lord because they honor Him.
He is wholly pure in His nature; being so, purity resonates with His righteous
expectations. This is why Jesus says, "The pure in heart ... see God" (Matthew 5:8).
Purity allows the lens of our soul to focus on our heavenly Father with clarity and
conviction. As we comprehend Christ's character, we are able to walk in His will. He
gives defined direction to clean hearts and minds.

However, sin soils our soul every day. I read something I should not read. I see
something I should not see. I hear something I should not hear. Our visual and
digital society seeks out unsuspecting souls and taints their thoughts. Stinking
thinking is detestable to the Lord. This is why we are compelled daily to confess,
"Create in me a pure heart, O God, and renew a steadfast spirit within me" (Psalm
51:10). Confession is cleansing.

"We demolish arguments and every pretension that sets itself up against the
knowledge of God, and we take captive every thought to make it obedient to Christ"
(2 Corinthians 10:5).

Indeed, there is a process for pure thinking. Are you a lazy thinker or an intentional one? How do you take captive every thought and align its allegiance to the
Almighty? Disciplined thinking avoids shallow, self-indulgent thoughts. Instead, it
prayerfully and unselfishly contemplates the depths of Christ's wisdom, love, and
holiness.

God gives us a diverse menu of rich thoughts from which to feast. "Whatever is
true, whatever is noble, whatever is right, whatever is pure, whatever is lovely, what-

ever is admirable—if anything is excellent or praiseworthy—think about such things" (Philippians 4:8). Do I ponder pure and pleasing thoughts to Him? My Master is a mind reader; so I make this my prayer:

"May the words of my mouth and the meditation of my heart be pleasing in your sight, O LORD, my Rock and my Redeemer" (Psalm 19:14).

Lord, I pray that my thoughts are Your thoughts. Fill my mind with Your wisdom.

Related Readings: Psalm 24:4; Isaiah 66:18; Matthew 9:4; Matthew 15:19

REFLECTIONS

_____

_____

_____

_____

_____

77

HOLY SPIRIT MOTIVATED

All a man's ways seem innocent to him,
but motives are weighed by the LORD.
Proverbs 16:2

Why do you do what you do? Is it for the glory of God or for the satisfaction of self? There is a subtle difference in serving with the Lord for His glory and doing our own thing, only mentioning Him as an afterthought. We cannot impartially judge our hearts, but Christ can. We are too close to be totally objective in our assessment of our actions and motives. However, the Holy Spirit has an effective way to weigh what we do.

Sometimes His way does not make sense. He has you in a fruitful situation, and then the Holy Spirit leads you to an overwhelming need with discouraged disciples. "The Spirit told Philip, 'Go to that chariot and stay near it.' ... Philip baptized him. When they came up out of the water, the Spirit of the Lord suddenly took Philip away, and the eunuch did not see him again, but went on his way rejoicing" (Acts 8:29, 38–39). Are you willing to leave a place where you are loved for an unknown initiative? Is your heart in it for Him and what is best for the kingdom, or is it about making your name known?

"By faith Abraham, when called to go to a place he would later receive as his inheritance, obeyed and went, even though he did not know where he was going" (Hebrews 11:8).

Jesus experienced this before His intense temptation with the devil. "Jesus, full of the Holy Spirit, returned from the Jordan and was led by the Spirit in the desert, where for forty days he was tempted by the devil" (Luke 4:1–2). Sometimes He leads us through the desert of temptation to purify our motives. Adversity prepares us to offer up the praise of people as a praise offering to the Lord. Indeed, gratitude to God gives Him the glory.

In reality, only God really knows the authenticity of your motivation. Furthermore, Holy Spirit motivation will sustain you to serve. Like the captain of a ship, you serve for the sake of the crew to keep the pirates at bay. Ponder, "Am I willing to do what I do without pay or for lesser pay for a period of time, or is money my true motive?" Therefore, start with pure prayers inspired by the Holy Spirit. Motive matters most to your Master.

"When you ask, you do not receive, because you ask with wrong motives, that you may spend what you get on your pleasures" (James 4:3).

Can I be content only with the consolation of Christ for my efforts?

Related Readings: Deuteronomy 9:4; 1 Samuel 16:7; Luke 16:15; 2 Corinthians 10:12

REFLECTIONS

_____

_____

_____

_____

_____

78

MORAL AUTHORITY

Kings detest wrongdoing, for a throne is established through righteousness.
Proverbs 16:12

Moral authority gives leaders the creditability to lead the most effectively. Presidents, judges, congressmen, governors, mayors, businessmen, teachers, preachers, and parents all require moral authority to be a leader worth following. It is the fabric of faith in God's standard that bolsters respect from followers. So what is your standard for conduct? Is your conscience governed by Christ's character? Is He your baseline of behavior?

If "everyone [does] what [is] right in his own eyes" (Judges 21:25 NKJV), there is cultural chaos and moral confusion. It may be a work culture that is inconsistent in its accountability or a home environment where the parents do not model the behavior they expect from their children. Rules are only followed consistently if righteousness rules.

"Who is wise and understanding among you? Let them show it by their good life, by deeds done in the humility that comes from wisdom" (James 3:13).

Your Creator has given you rights based on His righteous standard of behavior. If, however, we ignore the implementation of integrity, we forfeit our rights. God's gift of freedom is fragile and flourishes only in a faith-based society. Those ungrateful to God travel down a path of pride to their peril. "There is a way that seems right to a man, But its end is the way of death" (Proverbs 16:25 NKJV). Moral authority is accountable to almighty God.

Therefore, I have to ask myself: "Do I detest wrongdoing?" "Do I engage injustice with Christlike character?" "Do I compromise God's standards, or do I walk away from unseemly situations and shady deals?" The conscience of culture changes one heart at a time. Moral authority is the master of a leader's fate. With it comes creditability and the Lord's blessing, without it a shell of service at best, corruption at worst.

"Those who have served well gain an excellent standing and great assurance in their faith in Christ Jesus" (1 Timothy 3:13).

Do I lead with the moral authority of my Master Jesus?

Related Readings: 2 Samuel 23:3-4; 2 Chronicles 19:5-7; Luke 12:48; Revelation 19:11

REFLECTIONS

_____

_____

_____

_____

_____

79

PRIDE
BEFORE DESTRUCTION

Pride goes before destruction, a haughty spirit before a fall.
Proverbs 16:18

Pride is an entrée to destructive behavior. It facilitates foolish actions and is disparaging to relationships. Pride is not afraid to offend anyone and appeases no one. Its demanding spirit may gain short-term results under duress, but in the long-term people loathe its indulgent attitude. Indeed, do not fear pride in others; fear it in you yourself.

False humility is a subtle form of pride. "Do not let anyone who delights in false humility and the worship of angels disqualify you for the prize. Such a person goes into great detail about what he has seen, and his unspiritual mind puffs him up with idle notions" (Colossians 2:18). These are people who use spiritual talk to try to impress others with religious information. False humility speaks softly about its superior spiritual knowledge.

However, heaven is not idle in its attitude toward pride. It is pride that hurled Lucifer out of the presence of the Lord and into hell (see Isaiah 14:11–13). God runs out of patience with the proud of heart set in their ways. He brings down the stubborn and insubordinate. Because pride forgets God and marginalizes faith, He removes the self-absorbed.

"Before his downfall a man's heart is proud, but humility comes before honor" (Proverbs 18:12).

Therefore, humble yourself before God and man. Engage in extending and receiving forgiveness. Give Christ the credit for your accomplishments, and take responsibility for your failures. Humility honestly asks, "Do I care more about others than indulging myself? Am I a generous giver or a greedy getter?"

Replace haughtiness with humility, and the Lord will lift you up.

"For everyone who exalts himself will be humbled, and he who humbles himself will be exalted" (Luke 14:11).

Do I use my influence to further the success of others or to advance my agenda?

Related Readings: Leviticus 26:19; 2 Chronicles 26:16; Daniel 5:20; Luke 1:51

REFLECTIONS

_____

_____

_____

_____

_____

80

PLEASANT WORDS

Pleasant words are a honeycomb,
sweet to the soul and healing to the bones.
Proverbs 16:24

Pleasant words promote instruction and encourage people in the right direction. Like honey, these verbal morsels are sweet and satisfying to the soul. If you want to be attractive and influence others, use honey instead of harshness. Pleasant words please the Lord, bringing out the best in hungry hearts. A heart full of the Holy Spirit has the lovely language of the Lord at its disposal. Indeed, pleasant words are wrapped in prayer.

As you seek the Lord in prayer, He will show you what to say. Speech seasoned by God's grace offers eternal life and earthly energy. When you feed on the Word of God, your words take on strength and significance. The grace of God guards your heart to season your speech with the Spirit's sensitive candor.

"They are more precious than gold, than much pure gold; they are sweeter than honey, than honey from the comb. By them is your servant warned; in keeping them there is great reward" (Psalm 19:10–11).

Pleasant words provide direction and accountability. They create concrete conversations that are clear and compelling. Caring communicators do not speak at surface levels without risking to probe deeper, really making sure the listener understands. Use questions to clarify. Do not assume their answers are an accurate indicator of their understanding. Pleasant words are patient and take the time to confirm comprehension.

Lastly, sin disjoints our feelings and disconnects our faith. We need realignment and reconnection. Pleasant words reset broken bones of the soul and bring healing to the heart. If I read the transcript from my daily conversations, would I discover not only pleasant but profitable words? Your pleasant words bring healing and hope to the soul.

"Let your conversation be always full of grace, seasoned with salt, so that you may know how to answer everyone" (Colossians 4:6).

Are my words healing or hurtful to the ones who love me the most?

Related Readings: Deuteronomy 32:2; Psalm 119:103; Jeremiah 15:16; Titus 2:7–8

REFLECTIONS

_____

_____

_____

_____

_____

8 1

GOSSIP SEPARATES

A perverse man stirs up dissension,
and a gossip separates close friends.
Proverbs 16:28

Gossip is a friend of the insecure and unstable. It is easy for them to go there because it is comfortable and tantalizing. Gossiping makes the insecure feel superior. People with too much time on their hands are prime candidates for gossip because they are bored. For them it is sport to speculate on another's situation at that person's expense. They relish rumors.

However, gossips prey on God's patience. He can give them over to their depraved minds and categorize them with severe sinners. "They are gossips, slanderers, God-haters, insolent, arrogant and boastful; they invent ways of doing evil; they disobey their parents" (Romans 1:29–30). Gossips grieve the heart of God. They betray the Lord and His children. Idle and cheap talk fails to trust the Lord. Gossip is a serious offense.

"A gossip betrays a confidence; so avoid a man who talks too much" (Proverbs 20:19).

Therefore, it is best to avoid a gossip, not giving credence to his or her callous conversations. Indeed, we all have to watch our words lest we drift into stirring up dissension. "Did you hear about…?" is generally not a healthy phrase that produces productive outcomes. A friend talks with his friend, not about his friend. A brother does not gossip about a brother.

So the mature cease from speculating and only draw conclusions after hearing the facts. It takes more time and prayer to honor someone with your speech, but this is the way of the wise. Spirit-filled friends do not whisper behind another's back but speak frankly to his or her face. Do I use words to wound a friend's reputation or to help heal his or her heartache? Do my conversations with Christ followers separate or unify friends? Apathy is not an option for caring Christians. Love confronts personally and communicates with care.

"Brothers, if someone is caught in a sin, you who are spiritual should restore him gently. But watch yourself, or you also may be tempted. Carry each other's burdens, and in this way you will fulfill the law of Christ" (Galatians 6:1–2).

With whom do I need to speak face-to-face, not behind their back?

Related Readings: Proverbs 11:3; 26:20; James 3:5; 3 John 1:10

REFLECTIONS

_____

_____

_____

_____

_____

82

TEST OF TRUST

The crucible for silver and the furnace for gold,
but the LORD tests the heart.
Proverbs 17:3

The Lord tests the heart to build our trust. Resistance to our effort creates a reason to reach out to our Creator. Your test of trust is not a trivial pursuit but a process of purification. Like the cleansing crucible for precious metals, the Lord uses tests to extract the crude of our pride and replace it with the cream of His humility. Tests invite trust.

Indeed, the fruit of refining trials is faith. It may be a financial test you are facing. Will you spend less and give more as you watch your net worth shrink? You may have failed the relational test in your marriage, with your children, or with a parent. Be hopeful, for you can find success in failure. Failure strips away the nonessentials so all that is left is raw faith. Failure is not final. It is a stepping-stone for the Lord's work.

"For you, O God, tested us; you refined us like silver" (Psalm 66:10).

Testing is the Lord's tool to teach you trust. It may feel like the Holy Spirit has strip-searched your soul because you feel humiliated and exposed. Refinement is not always pleasant, but it is necessary to prepare you for success at work and home. The building of your character is Christ's way to prepare you for your next milestone of achievement. Fire fuels faith.

Lastly, affluence may be your greatest test of trust in God. The more you have, the less you feel you need the Lord. "You may say to yourself, 'My power and the strength of my hands have produced this wealth for me.' But remember the LORD your God, for it is he who gives you the ability to produce wealth" (Deuteronomy 8:17–18).

Have I passed the test of prosperity? Do I give Christ the credit for my accomplishments?

Related Readings: 2 Chronicles 32:21; Job 23:10; 1 Corinthians 3:13; 1 Peter 1:7

REFLECTIONS

_____

_____

_____

_____

_____

83

GIFT OF GRANDCHILDREN

Children's children are a crown to the aged,
and parents are the pride of their children.
Proverbs 17:6

There are privileges to maturing in age, and one of them is the gift of grandchildren. Like a king and queen's crown, their exceptional value is to be displayed proudly. You look at their hands and feet, and you pray for them to handle life prayerfully and to walk wisely with the Lord. You gaze into their innocent eyes and see glimpses of God's glory. You pray for them to look often to the face of Jesus and be loved by Him.

Grandchildren are a gift from God that invites love and unifies families. They are a reminder that the Lord is at work extending His legacy. So as you love these little ones, make sure to sow into them the Word of God, modeling grace, love, forgiveness, and fear of the Lord. Teach them to keep their eyes on Jesus because He will never let them down. Godly grandparents invite gullible grandchildren into their lives.

"But from everlasting to everlasting the LORD'S love is with those who fear him, and his righteousness with their children's children" (Psalm 103:17).

Invite them to your work so they can see how you relate to people with patience, encouragement, and accountability. Invite them into your home so they soak in your unconditional love and learn respect for their grandmother and grandfather. Make sure they catch you laughing out loud every time they visit with you. Call them on the phone; send them e-mails and birthday cards; take them on trips; buy them ice cream, clothes, and their first Bible. Make their memories with you bring a smile to their face.

Lastly, if you are a parent, honor your parents by allowing them to be in the presence of your children. Take a break from parenting, and let your mom and dad spoil them. If you are a grandparent, be extremely grateful to your children for the opportunity to invest in their children. Honor your children by respecting their way of parenting. Work with them, not against them. Indeed, your children still need your time, money, and wisdom.

"But from everlasting to everlasting the LORD's love is with those who fear him, and his righteousness with their children's children—with those who keep his covenant and remember to obey his precepts" (Psalm 103:17–18).

How can I be intentional in my time with my parents or grandchildren?

Related Readings: Psalm 78:4–6; 128:6; Proverbs 13:22; Joel 1:2–4

REFLECTIONS

84

MESSY ARGUMENTS

Starting a quarrel is like breaching a dam;
so drop the matter before a dispute breaks out.
Proverbs 17:14

Messy arguments are the result of fighting in the flesh. It is relational suicide, causing wounds that will not easily be forgotten. Anger is the primary driver behind messy arguments. Hard feelings cannot get around not being heard or not getting their way. For productive discussion over disagreements, level heads must prevail.

Spirit-filled followers of Jesus have the capacity to not only fight fair but also to disagree respectfully, while seeking to understand the other's point of view. If your mind is already made up, there is little possibility for positive relational results. Your friendship does not have to be sacrificed to make a point. In fact, people grow deeper in love and respect when they first bring their disagreements to the Lord, letting Him lead their lives.

"Brothers, choose seven men from among you who are known to be full of the Spirit and wisdom" (Acts 6:3).

Ask, "What does God think?" Because you do not argue with the Almighty, "Woe to him who quarrels with his Maker" (Isaiah 45:9). Bickering is marginalized when two people review God's game plan for disagreements (see Matthew 18:15–17). It may require involving an experienced, objective, and godly third party. If a neutral person is agreed upon, then the disputing individuals should follow the objective person's solution for resolution.

Lastly, once you make your point clearly, concisely, and maturely, you can trust the Lord and the responsible parties to do the right thing. Everyone is accountable; so actions sown will reap consequences good or bad. Untainted debate comes with respect and patience, understanding the other person's perspective. A pure heart prevents messy arguments.

"What causes fights and quarrels among you? Don't they come from your desires that battle within you?" (James 4:1).

How can I honor others, especially those with whom I disagree? Am I full of grace and truth in my communications?

Related Readings: Proverbs 13:10; Isaiah 58:4; 1 Corinthians 3:3; 2 Timothy 2:23–24

REFLECTIONS

_____

_____

_____

_____

_____

85

FOOLISH CHILDREN

To have a fool for a son brings grief;
there is no joy for the father of a fool.
Proverbs 17:21

Foolish children flail around, trying to find themselves. Typically, they are terrible at managing money because they have no concept of conservative spending and consistent saving. They look to mom and dad to bail them out. They desire from their parents a stimulus package without structure or accountability. Childish children become masters of manipulation and guilt by subtly saying, "If you really loved me..." to get their way.

This grieves the heart of their parents. Their father and mother want to do the right thing but become conflicted on defining "what is right." The dad may be firm and the mom more merciful; so it is imperative they are unified in their approach in how they love their rebellious child. They cannot allow Satan to drive a wedge of doubt between them. Jesus said, "[A] household divided against itself will not stand" (Matthew 12:25).

"The proverbs of Solomon: A wise son brings joy to his father, but a foolish son brings grief to his mother" (Proverbs 10:1).

Start with sincere and aggressive prayer for a loved one bound up in foolish behavior. Pray for the Lord to change you, giving you the grace and courage to offer an aggressive love based on the love of your heavenly Father. You can love the unlovely as you ought, only after receiving His unconditional love. Remember the joy you had when they came into this world as God's gift; so trust their Creator to bring them back to Christ. He can.

Lastly, confide in the Christian community regarding your sorrow and hurt. You may be surprised how many have suffered a similar fate. Move beyond the mistakes of the past, and focus on faith in the present. Turn your child over to the Lord's love and discipline. Pray your foolish child will grow fatigued from folly and return to faith in God. Thus, in hope of a celebration one day, you pray, "Christ, give me confidence to let them go and give them to You." Foolish children especially need the faithful prayers and love of their parents.

"'For this son of mine was dead and is alive again; he was lost and is found.' So they began to celebrate" (Luke 15:24).

Lord, help me to see my child like You see me, Your child, with patient love and compassion.

Related Readings: 2 Samuel 18:33; Proverbs 19:13–26; 2 Corinthians 2:3; 3 John 1:4

REFLECTIONS

_____

_____

_____

_____

_____

86

FOCUSED FOLLOW-THROUGH

A discerning man keeps wisdom in view,
but a fool's eyes wander to the ends of the earth.
Proverbs 17:24

Wise leaders focus on follow-through and do not wander around detached from the details. Details are stepping-stones to success. If ignored, they are stumbling blocks to failure. Discernment keeps you systematically focused on a sequence of tasks, assuring the implementation of every point in a project. You are wise when you promise less and deliver more. Indeed, focused leaders who follow through can be trusted with more.

If the leader is distracted by the next new idea, he will not have the energy or mental capacity to follow through with the most strategic pending project. It is a naïve leader who thinks he or she can delegate his or her way away from staying engaged in the execution of mission-critical initiatives. Every day and week your team needs to hear discerning questions from you that increase its accountability. Follow-through engages.

"David also said to Solomon his son, 'Be strong and courageous, and do the work. Do not be afraid or discouraged, for the LORD God, my God, is with you. He will not fail you or forsake you until all the work for the service of the temple of the LORD is finished'" (1 Chronicles 28:20).

How is the progress related to the agreed-upon timeline for completion? What obstacles are in the way, and how can they be removed? Is the cost of the project within budget? What did we decide, and who is responsible for its implementation? Wise leaders know enough of the details to know what questions to ask. You keep wisdom in view by focusing on a few mission-critical strategies. You bring clarity to the course of action.

Teams clamor to follow a wise leader who is focused on follow-through. So model the way by doing what you say. Your servant leadership facilitates follow-through for the team members. Become their barrier breaker, giving them the confidence to carry on. Follow-through creates creditability. Above all, focus on the Lord, and follow through with what He tells you to do. Faith follows through. Perhaps you say no more and yes less.

Jesus said, "Simply let your 'Yes' be 'Yes,' and your 'No,' 'No'; anything beyond this comes from the evil one" (Matthew 5:37).

Am I a leader worth following because I follow through? Can I be trusted with more because I have been faithful with what I have?

Related Readings: Psalm 119:37; Proverbs 15:14; John 7:17; 1 John 2:16

REFLECTIONS

_____

_____

_____

_____

_____

87

UNFRIENDLY FAITH

An unfriendly man pursues selfish ends;
he defies all sound judgment.
Proverbs 18:1

Why are some people unfriendly? Are they just shy, or is there selfish intent? If I am fearful of being embarrassed because of my words, the focus is all on me, not on Christ and others. I need to get over myself and get on with God. It is not about self but about selfless love of people. If Christ is the center of my thinking, then I totally trust Him to grow my social skills. Silence can send the wrong message.

If someone silently judges another without seeking to understand and clarify his or her position, conceit and arrogance follow. Conversely, friendliness facilitates a safe environment so relationships can emerge and grow in grace. However, an attitude of contempt tends to make matters worse by not extending grace and understanding.

"When wickedness comes, so does contempt, and with shame comes disgrace" (Proverbs 18:3).

An unfriendly face can release selfish signals. It repels warmth and rejects intimacy. What does the expression on your face communicate—acceptance or rejection? Do you invite others into your emotional space with a pleasant expression, or do you dismiss them with a face without feeling? Our looks are a translation of our heart. Therefore, be friendly and attractive so your faith in Christ can be expressed with grace and love.

A friendly countenance says you are open to hearing a person's hurts and fears. You are not easily frustrated because your focus is on serving, not being served. Friendly faith is forever reaching out, sincerely seeking to understand another's perspective. Does my attitude portray a friend of Jesus or a friend of the world? Friendly faith facilitates faith.

"Be ready to speak up and tell anyone who asks why you're living the way you are, and always with the utmost courtesy" (1 Peter 3:15 MSG).

Lord Jesus, create a countenance in me that reflects Your joy and pleasant presence.

Related Readings: Proverbs 16:21, 24; John 15:14–15; Philippians 2:3; James 4:4

REFLECTIONS

88

STRONG AND SECURE

The name of the LORD is a strong tower;
the righteous run to it and are safe.
Proverbs 18:10

The Lord is strong and secure. Satan and his demons cannot scale His fortress of faith. Fear is unable to flex its muscles and make God move off His point of protection. Our Savior Jesus Christ is not scared in the face of unholy alliances. His name is sufficient for the saints, for there is nowhere else to go. Peter declared this truth:

"Lord, to whom shall we go? You have the words of eternal life. We believe and know that you are the Holy One of God" (John 6:68–69).

So where do you go when you get frustrated and afraid? Do you have a safe place that guarantees wisdom and discernment? Or do you flounder in your faith, moving from one false figure of safekeeping to another, only to come up short and disillusioned? Pastors can declare the Word of God, but they are not one hundred percent reliable as a righteous resource. Employers who provide for our financial needs are an instrument of the Lord, but they are not a consistent source. Family and friends care, but they are not always there.

Only the Lord longs to always walk with you. Jesus said, "And surely I am with you always, to the very end of the age" (Matthew 28:20).

His name is a strong tower of rest and refuge; so you can take sanctuary when being pursued by questionable cohorts. Run to His righteous resting place for renewal and strength. This world saps our energy and endangers our soul, but Jesus brings us to life. He is your strong tower of trust and peace.

There is enough in God to take care of your every need. His tower of trust is impregnable and impenetrable. Go inside and stay awhile in intimacy with Him; then go back into the world, clothed in your battle fatigues of faith. You are strong and secure in the trustworthy tower of your Lord Jesus. Be confident in Christ and His amazing grace.

"Finally, be strong in the Lord and in his mighty power. Put on the full armor of God so that you can take your stand against the devil's schemes" (Ephesians 6:10–11).

Do I seek my Savior's security in the tower of His trust? Am I clothed in Christ's character and power, ready to engage the world?

Related Readings: 1 Samuel 17:45; Psalm 9:9–10; Matthew 1:23; Revelation 1:8

REFLECTIONS

_____

_____

_____

_____

_____

89

LISTEN TO LEARN

The heart of the discerning acquires knowledge;
the ears of the wise seek it out.
Proverbs 18:15

Daily life offers lessons to learn, but to benefit we have to be listening. It may be your financial planner who offers suggestions on how to better budget and save money, or it may be a fellow office worker with a warning to spend more time with your family. God sends us people every day as His emissaries of truth, but are we listening? Listeners are learners.

Moreover, the acquisition of wisdom is more than listening. It is being intentional to look for the right kind of knowledge in the right kind of places. If your goal is to understand the ways of God, then study Scripture, learning from the lives of His faithful followers. The teachings of the Bible come alive when lived out in real life. So ask people you respect what they think, and then apply their wisdom to your situation.

"Therefore consider carefully how you listen. Whoever has will be given more; whoever does not have, even what they think they have will be taken from them" (Luke 8:18).

Active procurement of principles for wise living is the strategy of the discerning. A humble heart for truth tends to listen intently, asking questions for clarification. The discerning are deliberate to experience what they are learning; so it becomes a part of who they are. For example, when a mentor meets with you to discuss marriage, do the same for another seeking soul so you will learn to serve as you are being served.

Lastly, never stop listening to learn. Wisdom is a lifetime education. In fact, as you grow older, you discover how much more there is to learn. Humility keeps you teachable and maturing. Perhaps you make it a goal to learn something new each day. Pray for the people who engage you in conversation, asking what you need to know from them.

Jesus said, "It is written in the Prophets: 'They will all be taught by God.' Everyone who listens to the Father and learns from him comes to me" (John 6:45).

Do I see a stranger as a spokesperson of the Lord? Above all, do I listen to God and learn from Him?

Related Readings: Deuteronomy 31:12; Malachi 2:7; Philippians 4:9; 2 Timothy 3:14

REFLECTIONS

_____

_____

_____

_____

_____

90

OVERCOMING
AN OFFENSE

An offended brother is more unyielding than a fortified city,
and disputes are like the barred gates of a citadel.
Proverbs 18:19

What happens when you offend another? How do you deal with the awkwardness? You probably feel embarrassed and regret saying or doing something that has weakened, even severed, the relationship. However difficult, there is a process of penetrating hurt feelings and healing the heart. The Lord's desire is for us to first work out relational differences on earth and then reconcile with heaven. The words of Jesus are clear.

Jesus said, "If you enter your place of worship and, about to make an offering, you suddenly remember a grudge a friend has against you, abandon your offering, leave immediately, go to this friend and make things right. Then and only then, come back and work things out with God" (Matthew 5:23–24 MSG). An offense is a huge obstacle, especially when you are ignorant of its occurrence. But ignorance is not an excuse.

"My son, if you have put up security for your neighbor, if you have shaken hands in pledge for a stranger, you have been trapped by what you said, ensnared by the words of your mouth. So do this, my son, to free yourself, since you have fallen into your neighbor's hands: Go—to the point of exhaustion—and give your neighbor no rest! Allow no sleep to your eyes, no slumber to your eyelids. Free yourself, like a gazelle from the hand of the hunter, like a bird from the snare of the fowler" (Proverbs 6:1–5).

When you approach an offended friend, be careful not to say, "If I offended you." Instead, own it by confessing, "I am so sorry I offended you." Though your offense may have been unintended, taking responsibility with humility and grace opens the door for forgiveness. Be patient, for his or her guard is up, and it will take time for a grudge to go away. Continue to slay the offended friend with severe kindness. Unconditional love lingers long.

Reconcilable differences become a hopeful example to others who face similar situations of relational severance. Pursue your insulted friend as Jesus pursued you, with unrelenting love. He said, "For the Son of Man came to seek and to save what was lost" (Luke 19:10). Persistent prayer and love melt away the cold bars of an offended heart.

"Therefore confess your sins to each other and pray for each other so that you may be healed" (James 5:16).

How can I humble myself and own what I did? Have I clearly confessed my sin and asked for forgiveness? Am I contributing to the healing process?

Related Readings: Genesis 27:41–45; Proverbs 16:32; Amos 1:11; 2 Timothy 2:22

REFLECTIONS

_____

_____

_____

_____

_____

How to Become a Disciple of Jesus Christ

Then Jesus came to them and said, "All authority in heaven and on earth has been given to me. Therefore go and make disciples of all nations, baptizing them in the name of the Father and of the Son and of the Holy Spirit, and teaching them to obey everything I have commanded you. And surely I am with you always, to the very end of the age." Matthew 28:18-20

Holy Scripture gives us principles related to becoming a disciple and to making disciples:

1 **BELIEVE**: That if you confess with your mouth, "Jesus is Lord," and believe in your heart that God raised him from the dead, you will be saved. Romans 10:9

Belief in Jesus Christ as your Savior and Lord gives you eternal life in heaven.

2 **REPENT AND BE BAPTIZED**: Peter replied, "Repent and be baptized, every one of you, in the name of Jesus Christ for the forgiveness of your sins. And you will receive the gift of the Holy Spirit." Acts 2:38

Repentance means you turn from your sin and then publicly confess Christ in baptism.

3 **OBEY**: Jesus replied, "If anyone loves me, he will obey my teaching. My Father will love him, and we will come to him and make our home with him." John 14:23

Obedience is an indicator of our love for the Lord Jesus and His presence in our life.

4 **WORSHIP, PRAYER, COMMUNITY, EVANGELISM, AND STUDY**: Every day they continued to meet together in the temple courts. They broke bread in their homes and ate together with glad and sincere hearts, praising God and enjoying the favor of all the people. And the Lord added to their number daily those who were being saved. Acts 2:46-47

Worship and prayer are our expression of gratitude and honor to God and our dependence on His grace. Community and evangelism are our accountability to Christians and compassion for non-Christians. Study to apply the knowledge, understanding, and wisdom of God.

5 **LOVE GOD**: Jesus replied: "'Love the Lord your God with all your heart and with all your soul and with all your mind.' This is the first and greatest commandment." Matthew 22:37-38

Intimacy with almighty God is a growing and loving relationship. We are loved by Him, so we can love others and be empowered by the Holy Spirit to obey His commands.

6 **LOVE PEOPLE**: "And the second is like it: 'Love your neighbor as yourself.'" Matthew 22:39

Loving people is an outflow of the love for our heavenly Father. We are able to love because He first loved us.

7 **MAKE DISCIPLES**: And the things you have heard me say in the presence of many witnesses entrust to reliable men who will also be qualified to teach others. 2 Timothy 2:2

The reason we disciple others is because we are extremely grateful to God and to those who disciple us, and we want to obey Christ's last instructions before going to heaven.

Meet the Author
BOYD BAILEY

Boyd Bailey, the author of **Wisdom Hunters Devotionals**,™ is the founder of **Wisdom Hunters, LLC**, an Atlanta-based ministry created to encourage Christians (a.k.a. wisdom hunters) to apply God's unchanging truth in a changing world. By God's grace, Boyd has impacted wisdom hunters in over 86 countries across the globe through the Wisdom Hunters daily devotionals, wisdomhunters.com devotional blog, and devotional books.

For over 30 years, Boyd Bailey has passionately pursued wisdom throughout his career in full-time ministry, executive coaching, and mentoring. Since becoming a Christian at the age of 19, Boyd begins each day as a wisdom hunter, diligently searching for truth in Scripture, and by God's grace, applying it to his life. These raw, unedited, "real time" reflections from his personal time with the Lord are now impacting over 85,000 people through the **Wisdom Hunters Daily Devotional e-mails**.

In addition to the daily devotionals, Boyd has authored devotional books: **Infusion**, a 90-day devotional; **Seeking Daily the Heart of God**, a 365-day devotional; **Seeking God in the Psalms**, a 90-day devotional; and several 30-day devotional e-Books on topics such as **Wisdom for Fathers**, **Wisdom for Mothers**, **Wisdom for Grads**, and **Wisdom for Marriage**.

In addition to Wisdom Hunters, Boyd is the cofounder and CEO of **Ministry Ventures**, a faith-based, non-profit ministry. He has trained and coached over 1000 ministries in the best practices of prayer, boards, ministry models, administration, and fundraising. Prior to Ministry Ventures, Boyd was the national director for **Crown Financial Ministries** and an associate pastor at **First Baptist Church of Atlanta**. Boyd serves on the boards of **Ministry Ventures**, **Wisdom Hunters**, **Atlanta Mission**, **Souly Business**, and **Blueprint for Life**.

Boyd received his bachelor of arts degree from **Jacksonville State University** and his master of divinity degree from **Southwestern Seminary**. He and his wife of over 30 years, **Rita**, live in Roswell, Georgia, and are blessed with four daughters and three sons-in-law who love Jesus, and two granddaughters, and a grandson. He and Rita like to hike, read, travel, invest in young couples, work through their bucket list, watch college football, serve in missions, and hang out with their kids and grandkids whenever possible.

Wisdom Hunters resources by
BOYD BAILEY

DAILY DEVOTIONAL
Sign up for free Daily Devotional e-mails at **WisdomHunters.com**

E-BOOKS & PRINT BOOKS
available at **WisdomHunters.com**

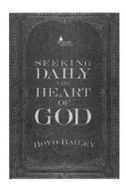

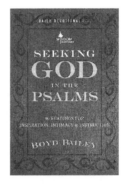

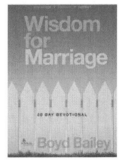

New **Wisdom Hunters App**
for iPhone and iPad on **iTunes.**

Free Download at iTunes!